School Composition for Use in Higher Grammar Classes

Writing in English, for Use in High Schools – Lessons on Language: Including Story Narration, Punctuation, Description, and Letter Writing

By William H. Maxwell

Published by Pantianos Classics

ISBN-13: 978-1-78987-167-8

First published in 1902

Contents

Preface .... *v*

Part I **7**
    Chapter One 7
    Chapter Two 13
    Chapter Three 20
    Chapter Four 27
    Chapter Five 34

Part II **42**
    Chapter One - Description 42
    Chapter Two - Narration 51
    Chapter Three - Exposition 61
    Chapter Four - Letter Writing 68
    Chapter Five - Versification 75

Part III - Paragraphs **78**
    Chapter One - Indention 78
    Chapter Two - Unity 82
    Chapter Three - Plan 87
    Chapter Four - The Topic Sentence 89

Part IV **94**
    Chapter One - Description 94
    Chapter Two - Narration 97
    Chapter Three - Exposition 100

Chapter Four 102

Chapter Five - Versification 109

Appendix I - Rules for Punctuation, Capitalization, and Spelling 113

Appendix II - Hints to Teachers on the Correction of Compositions 118

Preface

Much time and labor are expended in the higher grades of the grammar school in teaching children to write the mother tongue, but the results are far from satisfactory. The reason obviously is that fundamental principles are neglected, and that the efforts of teachers and pupils are in consequence misdirected.

To organize the teaching of English composition in grammar schools in accordance with certain principles, and to render pleasurable a task that is now irksome both to teacher and to taught, are the objects of this book.

The principles on which the lessons in the following pages are based are two: —

First, the child, like the adult, in order to become interested in what he writes, must write to instruct and entertain an audience. There is no such thing as writing well simply for the sake of writing. For the adult the audience is the public; for the child the audience is his class. It follows that the subjects upon which children will write with interest are subjects that appeal to children, — their occupations, games, the world of man and the world of nature as seen through childish eyes. Such are the topics suggested in this book.

Second, in order to learn how to be interesting, the child should be led to discover for himself the methods by which writers of note succeeded in becoming interesting, and then to imitate these methods. Hence the analysis and imitation of models constitute the staple of the book.

Upon these principles this volume has been constructed. Attention is also invited to the following features: —

1. The book is divided into four Parts, each Part comprising work sufficient for a term of five months.

2. The scheme of work is essentially inductive. In Part I children are taught to analyze models and to imitate them. In Part II the exercises are systematized under the heads of Description, Narration, Exposition, Letter-writing, and Versification. Part III is devoted to the paragraph. Not until Part IV is reached is an attempt made to gather the substance of the preceding pages into rules and definitions, which, all the way through, the young student has been discovering for himself.

3. The chief method employed in the study of models is the making of synoptic outlines, — an art in itself of incalculable value to whoever acquires it.

4. Exercises in the correct use of words and in the formation of typical sentences have been substituted for the exercises in the correction of faulty English usually found in books of this character.

5. Exercises in changing from the poetical to the prose sentence structure, in accordance with the method suggested by Professor Laurie, [1] have been substituted for the paraphrasing of poetry.

6. Teachers are requested to study carefully Appendix II on the correction of composition.

The selections from Burroughs, Bryant, Dana, Fiske, Hawthorne, Holmes, Lucy Larcom, Longfellow, Sill, Warner, and Whittier are published by permission of, and by special arrangement with, Messrs. Houghton, Mifflin, & Co., authorized publishers of their works. Acknowledgment is also made to Messrs. Harper & Bros., Charles Scribner's Sons, and Little, Brown, & Co. for permission to use various extracts from their several publications.

W. H. M.
E. L. J.

[1] "Lectures on Language," Sect. IV, by Professor S. S. Laurie.

Part I

Chapter One

Lesson One - How to Play Tee-Tah-Toe

This kind of "tee-tah-toe, three in a row," may have been in the first place an Indian game, as it is played with grains of Indian corn. A piece of board is grooved with a jack-knife, in the manner shown in the diagram.

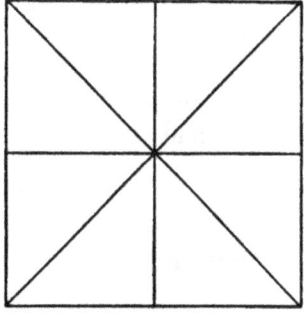

One player has three red or yellow grains of com, and the other an equal number of white grains. The player who won the last game has the "go," — that is, he first puts down a grain of corn at any point where the lines meet, but usually in the middle of the board, as that is the best place. Then the other player puts down one, and so on, until all the grains are down. After this the players move alternately along any of the lines, in any direction, to the next meeting-point of the lines, provided it is not already occupied. The one who first succeeds in getting his three grains in a row wins the game, and the board is cleared for a new game.

As there are always three vacant points, and as the rows may be formed in any direction along any of the lines, the game gives a chance for more variety of combinations than one would expect from the appearance of the board.

Adapted from "The Hoosier Schoolboy," by Edward Eggleston, Ch. V.

Study of the Model

If you had never played the game of "tee-tah-toe," you could do so after reading the foregoing explanation. That is because the writer has made perfectly clear to you what he had to say. Before he could write so clearly he must have thought clearly: he must have known exactly how this game is played.

If you read the model again, you. will find that each of its three paragraphs has its own work to do. The second is of the most importance, for it alone tells how the game is played. We might call this the *body* of the composition. The first paragraph introduces us to the game by telling us its name and the kind. It also tells what materials are used in playing it. The third paragraph glances back over the game that has just been explained, and tells what it is that makes it interesting.

If we write down in order the topics of these three paragraphs, we shall have the *plan* of the composition expressed as follows: —

    i. Introduction.
        1. Kind of game.
        2. Materials used in playing it.

  II. Body.
        How the game is played.
  III. Conclusion.
        Why the game is interesting.

Written Exercises

1. Write the model, from memory, using as a guide the plan given above.

2. Write an explanation of the way in which some indoor game is played. Select a subject from the list given below, or write about a game not mentioned here. 'Do not have an introduction if you think that your composition does not require one. Write as though you were explaining a game to a person who had never seen it played.

        Blindman's buff.   Ping pong
        Authors   Hunt the slipper
        Charades   Twenty questions

3. Write a similar composition on some outdoor game.

        Croquet   Cricket
        Baseball   Golf
        Lawn tennis   Basket ball

4. Make the meaning of the following sentences clearer by filling the blanks with suitable words.

Example. The game of tag always ___ and always will be popular.

The game of tag always has been and always will be popular.

a. In playing tag one runs as fast as he wants to ___.

b. In playing blindman's buff one should know better than ___ move about noisily.

c. Nowhere ___ is cricket played so much as in England.

d. No ___ rhymes are so well known by little children as those which they use in their games.

e. The game of authors and ___ of checkers exercise the mind rather than the body.

f. In playing checkers one person cannot have at first both the black and ___ white pieces.

g. The account of the cricket match in "Tom Brown at Rugby" is better than any ___ in literature.

h. John could not take part in the baseball game ___ Saturday; he was obliged to stay ___ home.

Lesson II - Grandfather's Chair

The chair in which Grandfather sat was made of oak, which had grown dark with age, but had been rubbed and polished till it shone as bright as mahogany. It was very large and heavy, and had a back that rose high above Grandfather's white head. This back was curiously carved in open work so as to represent flowers, and foliage, and other devices, which the children had often gazed at, but could never understand what they meant. On the very tiptop of the chair, over the head of Grandfather himself, was a likeness of a lion's head, which had such a savage grin that you would almost expect to hear it growl and snarl.

From "Grandfather's Chair," by Nathaniel Hawthorne, Ch. I.

Study of the Model

In this description Hawthorne has told us nothing about the arms, the legs, or the seat of Grandfather's Chair; because he is describing the chair as it appeared to the children when they stood at Grandfather's knee. They were deeply interested in the devices carved on the back of the chair and in the lion's head on the top. When they thought of the chair they thought of these things, and Hawthorne has so written this paragraph that when we think of Grandfather's Chair we also think of these things. We look at it with the children's eyes, or, to say this in another way, we look at it from the children's point of view. Nowhere in the paragraph has Hawthorne *said* that he is describing the chair as it appeared to the children, but we have only to read the description to see that this is the case. The children must have observed, —

1. What the chair was made of.
   a. Color.
   b. Polish.
2. Size and weight.
3. Back.
   a. Height.
   b. Carving.

Written Exercises

1. Write the model from memory.
2. Write a description of an easy-chair in your home. Write as though some member of your family is sitting in it as you look at it and describe it.
3. Write a description of the teacher's chair in your schoolroom. Contrast it point by point with Grandfather's Chair, using the outline given above. You might begin in this way: —

Our teacher's chair is not, like Grandfather's Chair, made of dark oak so highly polished that it shines like mahogany. It is made of —

4. Use the following words in describing chairs so as to explain the meanings of the adjectives.

Example. Grandfather's Chair was too massive to be moved easily.

luxurious	spacious
spindle-legged	upholstered
comfortable	enormous
rush-bottomed	wicker
antiquated	elegant
high-backed	inlaid
antique	durable
cane-seated	clumsy

Lesson III - Diary Kept at Fruitlands, 1843

September 1st — I rose at five and had my bath. I love cold water! Then we had our singing lesson with Mr. Lane. After breakfast I washed dishes, and ran on the hill till nine, and had some thoughts, — it was so beautiful up there. Did my lessons, — wrote and spelt and did sums; and Mr. Lane read a story, "The Judicious Father ": How a rich girl told a poor girl not to look over the fence at the flowers, and was cross to her because she was unhappy. The father heard her cross words, and made the girls change clothes. The poor one was glad to do it, and he told her to keep the clothes. But the rich one was very sad; for she had to wear the old clothes a week, and after that she was good to shabby girls. I liked it very much, and I shall be kind to poor people.

Adapted from "Louisa May Alcott: Her Life, Letters, and Journals," edited by Ednah D. Cheney. Little, Brown, & Company.

Extract from Hawthorne's "Note-Books"

March 31, 1851.

A walk with the children yesterday forenoon. We went through the wood, where we found partridge berries, half hidden among the dry, fallen leaves; thence down to the brook...I sat on the withered leaves at the foot of a tree, while the children played, a little brook being the most fascinating plaything that a child can have. Una jumped to and fro across it; Julian stood beside a pool, fishing with a stick, without hook or line, and wondering that he caught nothing. Then he made new waterfalls with mighty labor, pulling big stones out of the earth, and flinging them into the current. Then they sent branches of trees, or the outer shells of walnuts, sailing down the stream, and watched their passage through the intricacies of the way, — how they were hurried over in a cascade, hurried dizzily round in a whirlpool, or brought quite to a stand-still amongst the collected rubbish. At last Julian tumbled into the brook, and was wetted through and through so that we were obliged to come home; he squelching along the way, with his india-rubber shoes full of water.

From "Passages from the American Note Books," by Nathaniel Hawthorne.

Study of the Models

Here are two examples of the easiest kind of writing, — the telling in a plain, simple way, without attempting to make a story, the happenings of a day. To put down the incidents of each day in the order in which they occurred is to "keep a diary." This is an excellent way to train oneself to express one's thoughts easily.

The first selection is not entirely free from errors, but it is very well written for a girl of ten years. It gives an account of insignificant occurrences, but they were all that the healthy, happy, industrious little girl had to write about. By continued practice in trying to express her thoughts simply and naturally, this girl, when she grew older, was able to write "Little Women," "Little Men," and the other stories of Louisa Alcott's which you have enjoyed.

The second selection is taken from one of six volumes containing notes that Hawthorne made during a period of about twenty-five years. Wherever Hawthorne was — whether visiting some famous place in Europe or merely standing at a window of his own house in Salem — he found something worth looking at and writing about.

Written Exercises

1. Write an account of what you have done at home and in school to-day.

2. Suppose that you have spent one day doing exactly as you pleased. Write an account of the day.

3. Keep a diary for a week. Be sure to date each day's entry. Hand in the record a week from to-day.

4. Justify the use of *shall* and *will* in the following sentences taken from Hawthorne's "Grandfather's Chair." Read §404 of Maxwell's "Advanced Grammar."

Example. "Now I hope," said Charley, "we shall hear of his doing great things." *Shall* is used here because the speaker wishes to express mere futurity, not determination.

a. "But here are Lawrence, and Charley, and I," cried Cousin Clara, who was twice as old as little Alice. "We will all three keep wide awake."

b. "We won't go back empty-handed," said an English sailor; and then he spoke to one of the Indian divers: "Dive down and bring me that pretty sea shrub there. That's the only treasure we shall find."

c. "I shall remember this to-morrow," said Charley, "and I will go to State Street, so as to see exactly where the British troops were stationed."

d. "I am not like other historians. Battles shall not hold a prominent place in the history of our quiet and comfortable old chair. But to-morrow evening Lawrence, Clara, and yourself, and dear little Alice, too, shall visit the Diorama of Bunker Hill."

5. Write appropriate answers to the following questions, using *shall, will, should,* and *would.* Remember that the questioner uses with the second person the form that he expects to receive in the answer.

Example. Should you care to read the story called "The Judicious Father"? I should like very much to read it.

   a. Do you think you should have enjoyed taking a walk with Hawthorne?
   b. Should you recognize partridge berries if you should find them?
   c. Would you rob a bird's nest?
   d. Shall you use this book for two years or three?
   e. Shall you be glad when this lesson is done?
   f. Will you write this exercise very carefully?

Lesson IV

Elm Wood, Jane 11, 1849.

My dear Charlie, —

Let me assume the privilege of my uncleship to give you a little advice. Let me counsel you to make use of all your visits to the country as opportunities for an education which is of great importance, which town-bred boys are commonly lacking in, and which can never be so cheaply acquired as in boyhood.

Now, when you are at school in Boston you are furnishing your brain with what can be obtained from books. You are training and enriching your intellect. While you are in the country you should remember that you are in the great school of the senses. Train your eyes and ears. Learn to know all the trees by their bark and leaves, by their general shape and manner of growth. Sometimes you can be able to say positively what a tree is not by simply examining the lichens on the bark, for you will find that particular varieties of lichen love particular trees. Learn also to know all the birds by sight, by their notes, by their manner of flying; all the animals by their general appearance and gait or the localities they frequent.

I hope to hear from you again, and my answer to your next shall be more entertaining.

I remain your loving uncle,
J. R. Lowell.

From "Letters of James Russell Lowell," edited by Charles Eliot Norton, Vol. I.

Extract from One of Celia Thaxter's Letters

Yesterday when my brother and I were driving through the deep woods, following the track of the woodcutters who are making such carnage among the magnificent pines, we saw a bird, a wonderful bird. Near an open space where the lumber was piled (for there is a raving sawmill down there in the very heart of the woods), on the top rail of a fence, he alighted a moment close to us. He was larger than a robin, not so plump, but a good deal longer; his wings and tail were mottled black, white, and gray, but his whole body was the most delicious red color, all his feathers a kind of crimson and crushed-strawberry color, most vivid and delicate. We both thought his beak was roundish and blunt, something like a Java sparrow. We thought of crossbill and grosbeak, but it wasn't a crossbill, and I never saw a grosbeak so long and slender, and he was all over crimson, except his wings and tail. "Now what was he? Do tell us if you can.

Study of the Models

Notice that the poet Lowell advises his nephew to train his eyes while in the country. The writer of the second extract gives a good illustration of this eye-training. Only for a moment did the strange bird remain where it could be observed, but in that time Celia Thaxter observed all those points about its appearance which, when stated in her letter, enabled the naturalist to whom she wrote to name the bird for her. She noted: —
1. When and where the bird was seen.
2. Size and shape.
3. Color of wings, tail, and body.
4. Kind of beak.

Written Exercises

1. Write a reply to J. R. Lowell's. letter. First thank your correspondent for his good advice. Then carefully describe some peculiar plant or animal. Close the letter by asking for the name of the object described.
2. Write a letter to your teacher, describing minutely some bird you have seen or have read about. Write so that your teacher will recognize the bird you have described.
3. In your geography are probably many pictures of plants and animals. Write a letter to a classmate describing minutely one of these, and asking him or her to find in the book the picture you have used.
4. In connection with what animals is each of the following terms used? —

herd   covey   school   brace   flock   community   drove   brood   swarm
bevy   pack   flight

Chapter Two

Lesson V - How to Make and Manage A Float

The carriage we liked most was the "float." I have never seen it in the plays of other boys, though perhaps it is well known.
For a good float you want a board a foot wide, an inch thick, and four feet long. You want two rollers, which had better be of hard wood, each a foot

long and an inch or more in diameter; two inches would be better than one, but you take what you can get; a broomstick furnishes two or three good ones.

Placing these rollers two feet apart on the ground, you put the float upon them, with one roller at the end and the other in the middle. You then seat yourself carefully on the board, having two paddles in your hands, made from shingles. With these two paddles you will find that you can propel yourself over any floor of reasonable smoothness. You can even pass a threshold, and you can run into the most unexpected corners. If you have a companion on another float in the same room, you can have naval battles j or you can go to the assistance of shipwrecked crews. You can go forward or you can go backward, every now and then running a roller out, but skillfully placing it under the float at such an angle as will direct you in the way in which you wish to go afterwards.

For this game or sport you should not have too many companions; you should have a large attic or barn floor, and you should have unlimited patience. You can make a float, of course, out of a museum door, or out of any plank that happens to be going. I remember once, when we were hard pressed, one of my companions went to sea in a soap box. But what I have described is the ideal float for young people.

From "A New England Boyhood," by Edward Everett Hale, Ch. IV. Little, Brown, & Company.

Study of the Model

The author of "A New England Boyhood" did not wish merely to entertain his young readers by describing the plays and playthings of his own boyhood. He meant to make it possible for them to construct some of these playthings. Hence he has written very carefully this explanation of the making and the managing of a float.

In planning a composition of this sort it is a good idea to ask yourself the questions which a person ignorant of the subject might ask. Notice that the model answers in order the following questions: —

What is a float?
What materials are used in making it?
How is it managed?
What games can be played with it?

Written Exercises

1. Make an outline of the plan of the model, similar in form to the outline given in Lesson I, p. 8.

2. Make a similar outline for a composition on one of the following subjects: —

How to make and fly a kite.
How to put up a tent.
How to build a snow fort.
How to make a jack-o'-lantern.
How Robinson Crusoe made pottery.

How to enlarge pictures by squares.
How to make paper flowers.
How to make paper dolls.
How to hemstitch a handkerchief.
How to crochet a shawl.

3. Write a composition from your outline.

4. Fill the blanks in the following sentences with *this, each, all, either, neither,* or *both.*

a. As pleasant a trip may be made on a Crusoe raft as in ___ a rowboat or a sailboat.

b. Many rafts of ___ kind have been built.

c. ___ the logs are accurately measured.

d. ___ of them is trimmed and sharpened.

e. ___ the raft nor the scow-shaped rowboat is difficult to make.

f. — — of them is easily built by boys.

g. ___ are easily propelled, but ___ is good for a very long trip.

Lesson VI - Four Little Women

As young readers like to know "how people look," we will take this moment to give them a little sketch of the four sisters, who sat knitting away in the twilight, while the December snow fell quietly without, and the fire crackled cheerfully within. It was a comfortable old room, though the carpet was faded and the furniture very plain; for a good picture or two hung on the walls, books filled the recesses, chrysanthemums and Christmas roses bloomed in the windows, and a pleasant atmosphere of home-peace pervaded it.

Margaret, the eldest of the four, was sixteen, and very pretty, being plump and fair, with large eyes, plenty of soft, brown hair, a sweet mouth, and white hands, of which she was rather vain.

Fifteen-year-old Jo was very tall, thin, and brown, and reminded one of a colt; for she never seemed to know what to do with her long limbs, which were very much in her way. She had a decided mouth, a comical nose, and sharp gray eyes, which appeared to see everything, and were by turns fierce, funny, or thoughtful. Her long, thick hair was her one beauty; but it was usually bundled into a net to be out of her way. Round shoulders had Jo, big hands and feet, a fly-away look to her clothes, and the uncomfortable appearance of a girl who was rapidly shooting up into a woman and didn't like it.

Elizabeth — or Beth, as every one called her — was a rosy, smooth-haired, bright-eyed girl of thirteen, with a shy manner, a timid voice, and a peaceful expression, which was seldom disturbed. Her father called her "Little Tranquillity," and the name suited her excellently; for she seemed to live in a happy world of her own, only venturing out to meet the few whom she trusted and loved.

Amy, though the youngest, was a most important person, — in her own opinion, at least. A regular snow-maiden, with blue eyes, and yellow hair curling on her shoulders, pale and slender, and always carrying herself like a young lady, mindful of her manners.

From "Little Women," by Louisa M. Alcott, Ch. I. Little, Brown, & Company.

Study of Model

It was not the purpose of Miss Alcott to write such a description of the four sisters as an artist would need in order to paint their portraits. There are many details in regard to their appearance which she has left unnoticed. Her purpose was to give us only the most striking characteristics of their personal appearance, and to tell us just enough about their dispositions to make us feel toward them as she herself felt.

If you have read the book called "Little Women," you know that the author makes Jo the most interesting and original character in it, just as here she gives of Jo the fullest and most interesting description.

A very important thing to do in describing a person is to *select* the points that you will mention, making no reference to the points that will not help to produce the impression you wish to make on your readers. "Notice what points are mentioned in this description.

Margaret: age, figure, complexion, eyes, hair, mouth, hands.

Jo: age, figure, complexion, mouth, nose, eyes, hair, shoulders, hands, feet, clothes, manner.

Elizabeth: complexion, hair, eyes, age, manner, voice, expression, disposition.

Amy: age, complexion, eyes, hair, figure, manner.

Written Exercises

1. Write a description of two or more members of your family.

2. Write a description of some person with whose appearance the other members of the class are familiar. If you do not name the person, you can test the merit of your description by reading it aloud and seeing whether the class can name the person described. 3. Describe the appearance of one of the following characters as you would if you were talking to a child.

Cinderella	Aladdin
Little One Eye	Sinbad
The Sleeping Beauty	Tom Thumb
Little Three Eyes	Hercules
Santa Claus	Antaeus
Bluebeard	Mercury

4. Select from the following list those words that are suitable to use in describing (*a*) eyes; (*b*) noses; (*c*) mouths; (*d*) chins.

sharp	mobile
bright	determined
aquiline	keen

clear	sparkling
classic	laughing
smiling	upturned
receding	prominent
pointed	protruding
sensitive	firm
Roman	twinkling

Lesson VII - Home for The Holidays

I was roused from a fit of meditation by a shout from my three little traveling companions. They had been looking out of the coach windows for the last few miles, recognizing every tree and cottage as they approached home, and now there was a general burst of joy — "There's John! and there's old Carlo! and there's Bantam!" cried the happy little rogues, clapping their hands.

At the find of the lane there was a sober-looking servant in livery, waiting for them. He was accompanied by a superannuated pointer, and by the redoubtable Bantam, a little old rat of a pony, with a shaggy mane and long rusty tail, who stood dozing quietly by the roadside, little dreaming of the bustling times that awaited him.

I was pleased to see the fondness with which the little fellows leaped about the steady old footman and hugged the pointer, who wriggled his whole body for joy. But Bantam was the great object of interest; all wanted to mount at once, and it was with some difficulty that John arranged that they should ride by turns, and the eldest should ride first.

Off they set at last; one on the pony, with the dog bounding and barking before him, and the others holding John's hands; both talking at once, and overpowering him with questions about home, and with school anecdotes. We stopped a few moments afterward to water the horses, and on resuming our route, a turn of the road brought us in sight of a neat countryseat. I could just distinguish the forms of a lady and two young girls in the portico, and I saw my little comrades, with Bantam, Carlo, and old John, trooping along the carriage road. I leaned out of the coach window, in hopes of witnessing the happy meeting, but a grove of trees shut it from my sight.

Adapted from "The Sketch Book," by Washington Irving.

Study of the Model

Many writers would not have thought it worth their while to tell that when traveling in an English stagecoach they saw three boys returning home for the holidays, who were met by an old servant accompanied by a dog and a pony. This is an insignificant thing to tell. How is it that Washington Irving tells it in a way that makes us take an interest in the boys, and in old John, and Carlo, and Bantam? For one reason, he himself took a kindly interest in the boys, although they were only his fellow-travelers in a public coach. He showed his interest by leaning out of the coach window "in hopes of witnessing the happy meeting."

In choosing subjects for compositions observe this rule: Write about something in which *you* are interested.

Written Exercises

1. Reproduce the model from memory, but use the third person instead of the first; for example, use the words *Washington Irving* or *he* instead of *I*.
2. Write an account of some incident which you observed in a street car or other public conveyance. Do not invent any part of the incident.
3. Write an account of an incident which you observed on the school playground, on the street, or in a store.
4. Observe that the first word in each of the following groups of synonyms is taken from the model.
   a. Give the meaning which the words of each group have in common.
   b. Give the meaning which belongs to each word separately.
   c. Use each word so as to show its distinctive meaning.
   Example. Accompany, attend, escort.
   a. The words have the common meaning *to go with*.
   b. To accompany means merely to give one's company to; to attend means to go with in order to serve; to escort means to go with in order to protect or guard.
   c. We accompanied our friends to the station. The maid attended her mistress on the journey. The soldiers escorted the king to the palace.
   Rouse, awaken, stir up.
   Look, see, behold, view, eye.
   Cry, call, exclaim.
   Stand, stop, rest, stagnate.
   Doze, sleep, slumber, nap.
   Please, satisfy, gratify.
   Mount, rise, arise, ascend, climb, scale.
   Talk, speak, converse, discourse.
   Overpower, overwhelm, subdue.

Note. — Where it is necessary, the pupil should be allowed to consult a large dictionary, or a book of synonyms, such as that of Crabb.

Lesson VIII - A Letter

Vienna, Grand Hotel, November 19, 1882.
Very private!!

Dear Gertie, —

This letter is an awful secret between you and me. If you tell anybody about it, I will not speak to you all this winter. And this is what it is about. You know

Christmas is coming, and I am afraid that I shall not get home by that time, and so I want you to go and get the Christmas presents for the children. The grown people will not get any from me this year. But I do not want the children to go without, so you must find out, in the most secret way, just what Agnes and Toodie would most like to have, and get it and put it in their stockings on Christmas Eve. Then you must ask yourself what you want, but without letting yourself know about it, and get it too, and put it in your own stocking, and be very much surprised when you find it there. And then you must sit down and think about Josephine De Wolf and the other baby at Springfield, whose name I do not know, and consider what they would like, and have it sent to them in time to reach them on Christmas Eve.

Will you do all this for me? You can spend five dollars for each child, and if you show your father this letter, he will give you the money out of some of mine which he has got. That rather breaks the secret, but you will want to consult your father and mother about what to get, especially for the Springfield children; so you may tell them about it, but do not dare to let any of the children know of it until Christmas time. Then you can tell me in jour Christmas letter just how you have managed about it all.

Perhaps you will get this on Thanksgiving Day. If you do, you must shake the turkey's paw for me, and tell him that I am very sorry I could not come this year, but I shall be there next year certain! Give my love to all the children. Be a good girl, and do not study too hard, and keep our secret.

Your affectionate uncle,
Phillips.

Abridged from "Letters of Travel," by Phillips Brooks.

Study of the Model

Did Phillips Brooks mean that the secret he told to Gertie was really "awful"? He meant it just as much as he meant that Gertie was to be surprised at finding in her stocking the present which she herself put there, or that his message was to be delivered to the turkey. The writer of this letter knew that children like fun, and therefore, although he gave his niece exact instructions about the number and the price of the presents she was to buy, and told her also where she was to obtain the money for them, he did not write in the dry, formal way in which he might have written a business letter.

One of the rules for writing letters of friendship might be stated thus: Keep your correspondents in mind and try to write in a way to interest them.

Written Exercises

1. Answer the model letter. Date your letter sometime before Christmas Day. State when the letter was received. Send an imaginary message from the Thanksgiving turkey. Give an account of the buying of the presents, and tell how difficult it was to keep the secret from the other children.

2. Write a letter dated Christmas Day or the day after, giving an account of the distribution of the gifts.

3. Suppose that you have spent a holiday — Christmas Day, Thanksgiving Day, the Fourth of July, or Washington's Birthday — doing just as you liked. Write a letter to a friend, giving an account of the day.

4. Construct sentences beginning with the following clauses, and tell why the predicate verbs in these clauses are in the subjunctive mode. (See Maxwell's "Advanced Lessons in English Grammar," §§ 361-4.)

Example. If the Thanksgiving turkey were able to speak ___.

If the Thanksgiving turkey were able to speak, it might send a message to the children's uncle.

The predicate verb in the first clause is in the subjunctive mode to show that the speaker is expressing a condition which he knows is not true.

a. If the Springfield baby were able to write a letter ___.
b. If the children's uncle were here ___.
c. If some one were to give me five dollars ___.
d. If I were in Vienna now ___.
e. If I were you ___.

Chapter Three

Lesson IX - Invalids' Food

Of course we all know that the list of eatables allowed an invalid or a convalescent is of necessity a rather short one; but there is an infinite number of ways of varying the list, if one will use a little judgment and good taste in preparing the dishes. We have all had experience in seeing a sick person make a wry face at the mention of gruel or porridge, and precious little we blamed him for it, to tell the truth. But the whole condition of affairs may be changed by preparing it in this way; Have a pint of good clear chicken broth, free from fat and not too strong; boil it and into it shake slowly a cup of oatmeal or wheaten grits; let it cook for half an hour or so, pass it through a wire sieve, and add to it a little more broth if that is necessary to make it fit to be sipped easily from a cup without using a spoon. Take it to the sick-room with the remark, "I have brought you a little purée of oatmeal," and my word for it you will not see a drop left in the cup.

From "I Go A-Marketing," by Henrietta Sowle. Little, Brown, & Company.

Study of the Model

When a certain good cook was asked how to make the delicious scones (a kind of cake) for which she was famous, she replied, "Well, ma'am, you just take your griddle, and — and you make a scone." From this anecdote we learn that not every one who can do a thing is able to tell another person how to do it.

In this model we have exact directions for preparing a certain dish. Notice that the part beginning with, the words, "Have a pint of good clear chicken broth," consists of short, familiar words, not one word more or less than is necessary for the sense. This is the way in which to give directions for doing things.

The last sentence of the model might have been written thus: "Your patient will take all the broth if you do not call it by some commonplace name." This would have been saying the same thing, but in a less definite and lively way.

Written Exercises

1. Reproduce the model.
2. Write a recipe for making candy or anything else in the line of cooking that you earn make.
3. Write directions for cooking and serving a dinner of at least three courses, choosing your own bill of fare.
4. Fill the blanks in the following sentences with suitable prepositions. (See Maxwell's "Advanced Grammar," § 584.)

   a. Home-made bread is usually very different ___ bakers' bread.
   b. Sift the flour and salt together ___ a wooden bowl.
   c. Make a hole ___ the middle and pour ___ the yeast.
   d. Keep the jelly ___ the ice until you are ready to use it.
   e. Put the filling carefully ___ the layers.
   f. Pour another cupful of water ___ the teakettle ___ the pot.
   g, Take the pot ___ the fire and set it ___ the sink.
   h. The cook found that a good many beans had been scattered ___ the peas.
   i. Peel a small pineapple and cut it ___ strips.
   j. Let your patient sip the broth ___ a cup.

Lesson X - East's Study

Tom was for the first time in a Rugby boy's citadel. He hadn't been prepared for separate studies, and was not a little astonished and delighted with the palace in question.

It wasn't very large, certainly, being about six feet long by four broad. It couldn't be called light, as there were bars and a grating to the window; which little precautions were necessary in the studies on the ground floor looking out into the close, to prevent the exit of small boys after locking up, and the entrance of contraband articles. But it was uncommonly comfortable to look at, Tom thought.

The space under the window at the farther end was occupied by a square table covered with a reasonably clean and whole red and blue check tablecloth; a hard-seated sofa covered with red stuff occupied one side, running up to the end and making a seat for one, or, by sitting close, for two at the table; and a good stout wooden chair afforded a seat to another boy, so that three could sit and work together. The walls were wainscoted half-way up, the wainscot being covered with green baize, the remainder with a bright-patterned paper, on which hung three or four prints of dogs' heads. Over the door was a row of hatpegs, and on each side bookcases with cupboards at the bottom; shelves and cupboards being filled indiscriminately with schoolbooks, a cup or two, a mouse trap, and candlesticks, leather straps, a fustian bag, and some curious-looking articles which puzzled Tom not a little, until his friend explained that they were climbing-irons, and showed their use. A cricket bat and small fishing rod stood up in one corner.

This was the residence of East and another boy in the same form, and had more interest for Tom than Windsor Castle, or any other residence in the British Isles. For was he not about to become the joint owner of a similar home, the first place he could call his own?

Abridged from "Tom Brown's School Days," by Thomas Hughes, Ch. V.

Study of the Model

In the first paragraph of the model in Lesson VI there is a description of a room. It is, however, quite different from the description given here. Just enough is told about the room in which the four sisters sat knitting to suggest the plainness and the refinement of their home, — the cheerful fire, the good pictures; the books, the plants in the windows, suggest comfort and refinement; the plain furniture and the faded carpet suggest lack of wealth. The author gives this description of the room merely to help you to see the persons whose appearance she is about to describe. It is, as it were, the frame to the picture of the four sisters.

The model in this lesson gives a fuller description of a room. Tom Brown has just come to a school where he is to have a study of his own, and he is naturally much interested in the first room of the kind that he sees. He examines everything in it. Nothing escapes his eye, — he notices the barred window, the table covered with the red and blue cloth, the hard-seated sofa, the stout wooden chair, the pictures of dogs' heads on the walls, the contents of the cupboards, the cricket bat and the fishing rod standing in the corner, and even the hat-pegs over the door.

It is because the author is describing a Rugby boy's study from the *point of view* of a boy who is about to own a similar room, that he is so careful to mention the smallest details. If he were describing the room as seen by some grown person visiting the school for an hour or so, he might say: The room was small, poorly lighted, and furnished with the barest necessities of a study, — a table, a hard-seated sofa, a chair, and bookcases.

Why, in the first paragraph of the model, is East's room called a citadel? Was it really a palace? Why is the word *palace* used?

Written Exercises

1. Write a detailed description of your schoolroom. Write from the point of view of a pupil who is observing the room for the first time.
2. Describe such a room as you would like to have for your own at home.
3. Describe Sir Walter Scott's library as it appears in the picture on page 36.
4. Fill the blanks in the following sentences with nouns and pronouns in the possessive case. (See Maxwell's "Advanced Grammar," §§202-8 and §531.)

Example. There was no objection to a ___ furnishing his own study at Rugby, but the teachers did not like ___ indulging in much display.

Sir Walter Scott's Library at Abbotsford.

There was no objection to a pupil's furnishing his own study at Rugby, but the teachers did not like his Indulging in much display.

   a. The great charm of the Rugby boy's study consisted in ___ being his own.
   b. No one ever heard of the ___ having separate studies in our public schools.
   c. When we look at the picture of Scott's study, we do not wonder at ___ liking to write in such a room.
   d. ___ being a hard worker accounts for ___ having written so many books.

Lesson XI - The Wolf and the Lamb

As a Wolf was lapping the water at the head of a running brook, he spied a stray Lamb paddling, at some distance down the stream. Having made up his mind to seize her, he bethought himself how he might justify his violence.

"Villain!" he cried, running up to her, "how dare you muddle the water that I am drinking?"

"Indeed," said the Lamb, humbly, "I do not see how I can disturb the water, since it runs from you to me, not from me to you."

"Be that as it may," replied the Wolf, "it was but a year ago that you called me many ill names."

"Oh, Sir!" said the Lamb, trembling, "a year ago I was not born."

"Well," replied the Wolf, "if it was not you it was your father, and that is all the same; but it is no use trying to argue me out of my supper;" — and without another word he fell upon the poor helpless Lamb and tore her to pieces.

Aesop

Imitation - The Cat and the Bird

A cage with a Bird in it happened to be left on a low table in the room with a Cat. The Cat intended to eat the Bird, but thought he would first find a reason for doing so.

"What do you mean," he cried angrily, "by drinking all the milk in my saucer!"

"How could I get at the milk," said the Bird, sweetly, "when I am never allowed out of my cage?"

"Well," replied the Cat, "you are a trouble to me all the same, waking me in the night with your shrill singing."

"Oh, Sir!" said the Bird, fluttering, "I never sing until the sun comes in at the east window."

"If it is not you it is one of your relatives out of doors, replied the Cat, and, pulling the cage from the table, he ate up the Bird.

Study of the Model

For more than two thousand years Aesop's fables have been read and told. How does a fable differ from other stories? A fable is told for the purpose of making clear some truth about conduct. Instead of merely saying, "Self-help is the best help," Aesop tells the story of the lark and her young ones; instead of saying. "Learn to use your bright wits," he tells the story of the crow and the pitcher. In the majority of Aesop's fables, though not in all, the characters are animals that talk and act like human beings.

In the imitation of the fable here given, notice that the lesson taught is the same as that taught by the original fable, namely, that when a person means to do a wrong thing he can easily make excuses for his action.

Instead of having a bird and a cat for the characters in this imitation, would it have been as well to have a bird and a horse? No, because it would not be natural for a horse to eat a bird. In writing imitations of fables, let your characters, as far as possible, do what would be natural for them to do.

Written Exercises

1. Write another imitation of the fable "The Wolf and the Lamb." If you wish, you may use one of the following titles. Be careful of punctuation in writing the dialogue carried on by your two characters.

a. The Hen and the Worm.
b. The Shark and the Bluefish.
c. The Hawk and the Young Bird.

2. Write an imitation of "The Dog and His Shadow." Instead of a dog crossing a bridge with a piece of meat in his mouth, have a crane standing in shallow water with a fish in his bill.

3. Write an imitation of "Hercules and the Wagoner." The following suggestions may help you.

a. A boy's hat is carried by the wind to a stone in the middle of a narrow stream — boy calls to farmer for help — farmer tells him how to help himself.

b. A woman loses a gold piece on the floor of her room — sits down on her doorstep and cries to her neighbors for help — neighbors reply.

4. Select one of the following fables of Aesop for imitation. Use the suggested title or invent one for yourself.

Aesop	Imitation
1. The Crow and the Pitcher.	1. The Ant and the Large Crumb of Bread.
2. The Lark and her Young Ones.	2. The Chimney Swallow and her Young Ones.
3. The Fox and the Grapes.	3. The Cat and the Robin.
4. The Ants and the Grasshoppers.	4. The Squirrels and the Sparrows.
5. The Hare and the Tortoise.	5. The Snail and the Toad.
6. The Birds, the Beasts, and the Bat.	6. The Plants, the Animals, and the Venus's Fly-trap.
7. The Country Mouse and the City Mouse.	7. The Country Dog and the City Dog.
8. The Fox who had lost his Tail.	8. The Dog with Cropped Ears.

5. Make the meaning of the following sentences clear by using nouns in place of the obscure pronouns, by quoting the speaker s exact words, or by recasting the sentences. (See Maxwell's "Advanced Grammar," §§ 632-3.)

Example. The Fox told the Goat that if he would put his forefeet high up on the wall, he could get out of the well and could then help him out.

The Fox said to the Goat, "If you will put your forefeet high up on the wall, I can get out of the well and can then help you out."

a. The Crane told the Wolf that if he would lie on his side and open his jaws as wide as he could, he would try to take the bone out of his throat. This he did, and his neck was so long it was soon loosened and came out. When he wondered what reward would be given him, the Wolf showed his teeth and told him that as he had put his head inside of his mouth and taken it out in safety, he had had reward enough.

b. The Serpent said to the Farmer that he could never forget the loss of his son, nor could he forget the loss of his tail.

c. The Kid told the Wolf that he was a murderer and a thief, and he wondered what he was doing near honest men's houses.

d. The Fox said that he did not care to go into the Lion's cave until he had seen the animals that he had enticed into it come out of it.

Lesson XII

Staten Island, July 21, 1843.

Dear Helen, —

I have pretty much explored this island, inland and along the shore, finding my health inclined me to the peripatetic philosophy. I have visited telegraph stations, sailors' snug harbors, seamen's retreats, old elm trees, where the Huguenots landed, Britton's mills, and all the villages on the island....

I believe I have not told you anything about Lucretia Mott. It is a good while ago that I heard her at the Quaker Church in Hester Street. She is a preacher, and it was advertised that she would be present on that day. I liked all the proceedings very well....They do nothing in a hurry. Every one that walks up the aisle in his square coat and expansive hat has a history, and comes from a house to a house. The women come in one after another in their Quaker bonnets and handkerchiefs, looking like sisters or so many chickadees. After a long silence — waiting for the Spirit — Mrs. Mott rose, took off her bonnet and began to utter very deliberately what the Spirit suggested. ... It was a good speech....She sat down at length, and, after a long and decorous silence, in which some seemed really to be digesting her words, the elders shook hands. and the meeting dispersed. On the whole, I liked their ways and the plainness of their meeting house. It looked as if it was indeed made for service.

Tell all my friends in Concord that I do not send my love, but retain it still.

Your affectionate brother,

H. D. T.

Abridged from "Letters to Various Persons," by Henry D. Thoreau.

Study of the Model

This letter is very different in style from Phillips Brooks's letter given in Lesson VIII. It was written to an older person, and is mainly about a sober subject — a Quaker meeting. But the two letters are similar in this respect — that their writers have chosen topics which they thought would interest their correspondents. Thoreau's sister had probably never attended a Quaker meeting, and was therefore glad to read about the service, the preacher, and the congregation.

Written Exercises

1. Write from memory Thoreau's account of a Quaker meeting.
2. Write to a member of your family who has been away from home for a long time, giving an account of some new experience you have had, such as attending an entertainment.

3. Write as though you were away from home, giving an account of some interesting experience.

4. Write to a schoolmate who has been detained at home by sickness. Give an account of some school entertainment.

5. Fill the blanks in the following sentences with pronouns, being careful to employ the proper case-forms. (See Maxwell's "Advanced Grammar," § 589.)

a. ___ do you think I saw yesterday?
b. ___ do you suppose has been visiting us?
c. Mrs. A. sent my sister and ___ tickets for the concert.
d. My sister was ready sooner than ___.
e. I did not at once recognize Mrs. L., but as soon as she began to sing I knew it was ___.
f. Mr. G. ___, you used to know, sang a solo.
g. Between you and ___, it was not a great success.

Chapter Four

Lesson XIII - Learning to Swim

The swimming school was in water which flowed where Brimmer Street and the houses behind it are now built. It was just such a building as the floating baths are now which the city maintains, but that it inclosed a much larger space. Of this space a part had a floor so that the water flowed through; the depth was about five feet. To little boys like me it made little difference that there was this floor, for we could be as easily drowned in five feet of water as if there were fifteen...

As soon as you were undressed and ready — and this meant in about one minute — you took your turn to be taught. A belt, was put around you under your arms; to this belt a rope was attached, and you were told to jump in. You jumped in and went down as far as gravity chose to take you, and were then pulled up by the rope. The rope was then attached to the end of a long belt, and you were swung out upon the surface of the water. Then began the instruction.

"O-n-e, — two, three;" the last two words spoken with great rapidity, "one" spoken very slowly. This meant that the knees and feet were to be drawn up very slowly, but were to be dashed out very quickly, and then the heels brought together as quickly.

Boys who were well built for it and who were quick, learned to swim in two or three lessons. Slender boys and little boys who had not much muscular force — and such was I — were a whole summer before they could be trusted without the rope. But the training was excellent, and from the end of that year till now I have been entirely at home in the water.

From "A New England Boyhood," by Edward Everett Hale, Ch. III.

Study of the Model

If some one should write an explanation of the common method of instruction employed in the ordinary swimming school, he would probably give us the same information that the writer of this model gives. But the treatment of the subject would be quite different. Edward Everett Hale tells us, not how swimming lessons are generally given, but how he was taught to swim as a boy of nine years. This concrete way of treating a subject is the best for young writers to employ.

The topics of the four paragraphs of the model may be expressed as follows: —

I. The school.
II. Preparation for lessons.
III. Method of instruction.
IV. Results of instruction.

Under each we might have two or more subordinate topics. For instance, under I we might have, —

1. Situation.
2. Kind of building.
3. Depth of water.

Written Exercises

1. Complete the above outline by giving subordinate topics for the last three paragraphs.
2. Make a similar outline for a composition on one of the following subjects: —

Learning to skate.
Learning to ride a bicycle.
Learning to play on a musical instrument.
Learning to cook.
Learning to sew.
Learning to dance.
Learning to read.

3. Write the composition you have planned.
4. Fill the blanks in the following sentences with the proper forms of the verbs given in parentheses.

   a. A small boy can be ___ in five feet of water as easily as in fifteen. (drown)
   b. Who has ___ you to swim so well? (teach)
   c. Have you ever ___ more than a mile without resting? (swim)
   d. Had you ___ lessons when you did this? (take)
   e. What words were ___ by the teacher of swimming? (speak)
   f. The knees were ___ up very slowly. (draw)

5. Construct sentences containing the perfect participles of the i verbs used in the preceding exercise.

Lesson XIV - Spring Jottings

March 3, 1879. The sun is getting strong, but winter still holds her own. No hint of spring in the earth or air. No sparrow or sparrow-song yet.

March 5. The day warm and the snow melting. The first bluebird note this morning. How sweetly it dropped down from the blue overhead!

March 10. A real spring day at last, and a rouser! Thermometer between 50° and 60° in the coolest spot. The bluebirds! It seemed as if they must have been waiting somewhere close by for the first warm day, like actors behind the scenes, for they were here in numbers early in the morning; they rushed upon the stage very promptly when their parts were called.

March 12. A change to more crispness and coolness, but a delicious spring morning. The air is full of bird voices. A few days ago, not a bird, not a sound; everything rigid and severe; then in a day the barriers of winter gave way, and spring comes like an inundation.

Adapted from "Spring Jottings" in "Riverby," by John Burroughs.

Study of the Model

In the introduction to his "Spring Jottings" John Burroughs says, "For ten or more years past I have been in the habit of jotting down, among other things in my note-book, observations upon the seasons as they passed." Farther on he says, "When we try to tell what we saw or felt, even to our journals, we discover more and deeper meanings in things than we had suspected."

The jottings given here were written by a person living in the country. If you too live in the country, it will be easy for you to make similar notes, recording your observations of the weather, the arrival and the departure of the birds, the opening of the flowers, etc. But if you live in the city, you should not consider it impossible to make daily records of observations of nature. The weather is just as variable in the city as in the country. The sky with its clouds is not completely hidden from the eyes of city folk, who can, if they will, observe many natural signs of the changing seasons. It is recommended to every pupil to begin at once to keep such a note-book.

Written Exercises

1. Write a description of to-day, mentioning the temperature at a certain time, the condition of the atmosphere, and the appearance of the sky.

2. Keep a weather record for a week, handing it in one week from to-day.

3. Keep a three months' record of the signs of the seasons, not making notes every day, but only when some new sign has been observed.

4. Fill the blanks in the following sentences with the proper forms of the verbs *lie, lay, sit,* and *set.*

a. The breath of spring is in the air, but snow still ___ on the meadows.

b. This March came in like a lamb and went out like a lamb, thus ___ the old adage at naught.

c. Where the last remnants of the snowdrifts ___ yesterday, the plow breaks the sod to-day.

d. Flaky ice incrusts the borders of the pools, but here is our summer bee ___ up its store of pollen.

e. The little bird ___ at his door in the sun.

f. These brown leaves have ___ under the trees all winter.

g. We have had a succession of genuine Indian-summer days, with gentle winds or none at all, and a misty atmosphere, which idealizes all nature, and a mild beneficent sunshine, inviting one to ___ down in a nook and forget all earthly care.

Lesson XV - An Accident

One day my sister and I were allowed to take a walk together; I, as the elder, being supposed to take care of her. Although we were only going toward the Cove, over a secluded road, she insisted upon wearing a brand-new pair of red morocco boots.

All went well until we came to a bog by the roadside, where sweet flag and cat-tails grew. Out in the middle of the bog, where no venturesome boy had ever attempted their seizure, there were many tall, fine-looking brown cat-tails growing. She caught sight of them, and before I saw what she was doing, she had shot from my side like an arrow from the bow, and was far out on the black, quaking surface, that at first upheld her light weight.

I stood petrified with horror. I knew all about that dangerous place. I had been told that nobody had ever found out how deep that mud was. I had uttered just one imploring "Come back!" when she turned to me with a shriek, throwing up her arms toward me. She was sinking! There was nobody in sight, and there was no time to think. I ran, or rather flew across the bog, with just one thought in my mind, "I have *got* to get her out!"

Some angel must have prevented me from taking a misstep and sinking with her. I felt the power of a giant suddenly taking possession of my small frame. Quicker than I could tell of it, I had given one tremendous pull (she had already sunk above her boot-tops), and had dragged her back to the road. It is a marvel to me now how I — a child of scarcely six years — succeeded in rescuing her. It did not seem to me as if I were doing it myself, but as if some unseen Power had taken possession of me for a moment, and made me do it.

We were two miserable looking children when we reached home, the sticky ooze having changed her feet into unmanageable lumps of mud, with which my own clothes also were soiled. I had to drag or carry her all the way, for she could not or would not walk a step. And alas for the morocco boots! They were never again red. 1 also received a scolding for not taking better care of my little sister, and I was not very soon allowed again to have her company in my rambles.

Adapted from "A New England Girlhood," by Lucy Larcom, Ch. V.

Study of the Model

Lucy Larcom relates here one of her actual experiences, but, because she understands how to do it, she makes a real *story* of it. Now, a story has a *plot*, that is, its parts are arranged so as to arouse the reader's interest concerning the way in which it will end or the way in which things will turn out.

No matter how simple the plot, there is always some incident that is more important than the others. Here the important incident is the little girl's sinking in the bog. Notice how all that goes before is connected with this. What have the red shoes to do with the sinking? What has Lucy's being the elder sister to do with it? What has the position of the cat-tails to do with it? What have the height and the fine appearance of the cat-tails to do with it? And then notice how all that follows the sinking is connected with it — the elder sister's feelings, her unnatural strength, the muddy shoes and clothes, and the punishment.

Following is an outline of the story: —
1. Two little sisters set out for a walk.
2. They come to a bog where cat-tails are growing.
3. The younger child tries to cross the bog.
4. She begins to sink.
The older sister drags her back to the road.
5. The younger girl's new red shoes are ruined. The older child receives a scolding for not taking better care of her little sister. In writing a story, have your plot well in mind. Choose your main incident, and then let everything else you tell either lead up to this incident or result from it. Be sure to make your main incident the most important thing in the story.

Written Exercises

1. Reproduce the story from memory, using the third person instead of the first.
2. Outline the plot of some other story you have read.
3. Outline the plot for a story, using one of the following titles: —
   a. Meddlesome Matty.
   b. Lost and Found.
   c. A Little Hero.
   d. A Runaway.
   e. A Wise Old Horse.
4. Write a story, using one of the following plots: —
   a. The boys of a certain village were having a snow battle. From the beginning it appeared that one side was weaker than the other and occupied the poorer position on the battlefield; but, just as all hope seemed lost, the leader of this side made a clever move, by which he and his followers gained the victory. After the battle, a statue made of snow was erected in honor of the victorious leader.

b. The parents of a certain little girl nicknamed her Dillydally, because she never obeyed promptly. One day this bad habit was the means of her losing a pet animal.

c. For some reason, the mother of a thin, little, shivering colt would not take care of him. When he was several days old, Britta, another horse on the same farm, adopted him. There was a battle royal before Lassie, Britta' s own colt, would accept Laddie as her foster brother; but now Lassie and Laddie have become a fine team, known far and wide as Britta's twins.

d. Dame Duck was proud of her five children, but she did not take very good care of them. One of them was run over by a wagon wheel while chasing crickets around a haystack; a second scrambled into a pan of cold water, and was drowned; a third was caught in a trap set for rats; and the other two, having become fine, fat fellows, were eaten by the farmer's family.

Lesson XVI

Braintree, June 18, 1775.

My dearest Friend,

The day — perhaps the decisive day — has come, on which the fate of America depends. I have just heard that our dear friend. Dr. Warren, is no more, but fell gloriously fighting for his country. Great is our loss. He has distinguished himself in every engagement by his courage and fortitude, by animating the soldiers, and leading them on by his own example.

Charlestown is laid in ashes. The battle began upon our intrenchments upon Bunker Hill, Saturday morning, about three o'clock, and has not ceased yet, and it is now three o'clock. Sabbath afternoon.

It is expected they will come out Over the Neck to-night, and a dreadful battle must ensue. How many have fallen we know not. The constant roar of the cannon is so distressing that we cannot eat, di-ink, or sleep.

I shall tarry here till it is thought unsafe by my friends, and then I have secured a retreat at your brother's, who has kindly offered me part of his house. I cannot compose myself to write any. further at present. I will add more as I hear further.

I am most sincerely yours,
Portia.

Adapted from "Familiar Letters of John Adams and his Wife, Abigail Adams."

Study of the Model

This letter is a copy, shortened somewhat, of one written to John Adams, who became the second president of the United States. The writer, Mrs. Adams, was living near Boston when the battle of Bunker Hill occurred, and her husband was in Philadelphia attending a meeting of the Continental Congress.

The letter interests us because it was written by one who was actually within sound of the battle. It makes the far-off event seem real and near to us. But we do not expect to get from a letter of this kind the full and correct account of the battle which we can find in any good history. It is usually not until long after a battle has taken place that a complete account of it can be written.

Compare this real letter written while the battle was actually taking place with Oliver Wendell Holmes's poem, "Grandmother's Story of Bunker Hill Battle." The latter is a detailed account of the same event supposed to be given by an old lady who, when a young girl, saw the battle from a belfry in Boston.

Written Exercises

1. Imagine yourself a son or a daughter of one of the farmers of Middlesex, Massachusetts, who took part in the battle of Lexington. Write a letter, dated April 19, 1775, giving some friend an account of how Paul Revere warned your father of the approach of the British. (Read Longfellow's "Paul Revere's Ride.")

2. Write another letter, dated April 20, 1775, giving an account of the battle as related to you by your father.

3. Write one of the following: —

a. A letter, dated December 26, 1776, from an eye-witness of Washington's famous victory at Trenton on Christmas Day.

b. A letter from Yorktown, dated October 19, 1781, giving an account of the siege, and of the surrender of Cornwallis.

c. A letter from New Orleans, dated January 8, 1815, giving an account of Jackson's defense of the city.

d. A letter from a sailor who was serving under Perry when he won his great victory on Lake Erie.

e. A letter from a sailor who was serving under Admiral Dewey when he won his victory on Manila Bay.

f. A letter from one of Stonewall Jackson's soldiers, giving an account of Barbara Frietchie's heroic deed. (Read Whittier's poem, "Barbara Frietchie.")

4. Put in their proper places in the following sentences the words that are in parentheses. If they can be placed in more than one position, explain the difference in the meanings of the resulting sentences. Read §§ 596 and 597 of Maxwell's "Advanced Lessons in English Grammar."

a. I should not like to see a battle, (very much)
b. The roar of the cannon told that the battle had begun, (only)
c. The soldiers, after firing, threw themselves on the ground to reload, (hastily)
d. At the English right a fire was kept up by sharpshooters from the bushes and cornfields, (chiefly)
e. The troops began to retreat, (rapidly)
f. All who fought were heroes, (not).
g. Washington's victory appeared miraculous, (almost)

5. Construct sentences containing the correlatives *not only ... but, both ... and, neither ... for, and either ... or.*

Be sure to place each member of a pair before the same part of speech.

Example. Montcalm was blamed not only for fighting too soon, but for fighting at all.

Chapter Five

Lesson XVII - Winter Fishing

Those screens of sailcloth fastened to two poles, which I see every winter from my parlor windows, recall the old delight of boyish days, in fishing through the ice. It was not sport of a lofty order, but it had a pleasure in it for unsophisticated youth, to whom the trout was an unknown animal and the fly a curious thing to read about in "The Complete Angler." This is, or was, the order of winter fishing.

Your tackle shall be a heavy sinker, with a wire running through it, with a hook suspended to each end of the wire. The end of your line shall be fastened to one end of a half parenthesis of wooden hoop), the other being thrust into a hole just at the edge of the opening of the ice through which you fish. Your bait is a most ill-favored, flat, fringed, naked worm, dug out of the mud of the river bank.

Plump go sinker and baited hooks through the oblong square opening, down, down, until the line hangs straight from the end of the curved elastic hoop. Presently bob goes the hoop, — bob, — bob, — bob, — bob, — b — b — b — b! Pull up, pull up! Oo! Oo! how cold! ...

I cannot make this river fishing as poetical as Thoreau has made pickerel fishing on Walden, yet it is not without its attractions. The crunching of the ice at the edges of the river as the tide rises and falls, the little cluster of tentlik^ screens on the frozen desert, the excitement of watching the springy hoops, the mystery of drawing up life from silent unseen depths, and the rivalry with neighboring fishermen, are pleasant recollections enough to account for the pains often taken with small result.

From "Pages from an Old Volume of Life," by O. W. Holmes.

Study of the Model

"The Complete Angler" mentioned in the first paragraph of the model, was the first book of importance ever written on the art of fishing. Its author was Isaac Walton, an Englishman born in 1593. He set a fashion that has been followed by innumerable writers. No other form of sport has been so much written about as fishing.

Read the second and third paragraphs of the model. Observe that Dr. Holmes, although really giving you an explanation of the way in which boys fished through the ice in his young days, pretends that you, the reader, are doing the fishing now, and that he is at your elbow telling you how to do it. By this means he makes his explanation clear and, at the same time, lively and entertaining.

Read the last paragraph. Observe how clearly Dr. Holmes has enumerated in one sentence (the second) the five things that made this kind of fishing attractive. The sentence is longer than the sentences young writers should use until they have had considerable practice in writing, but it is a very good kind of sentence to learn how to make.

Written Exercises

1. Outline the plan of the model.
2. Write an explanation of the manner in which you have fished, or in which some person you have observed has fished.
3. Reproduce an account of fishing which you have read.
4. Put in their proper places in the following sentences the phrases that are in parentheses. This direction means that you should place them as near as possible to the words they modify. Before writing this exercise you should study the rules for the use of the comma in Appendix I, and you should read again §§ 596 and 597 of Maxwell's "Advanced Lessons in English Grammar."

a. You never get so close to the birds as when you are wading quietly down a little river. (Casting your fly deftly under the branches. For the wary trout.)

b. The spotted sandpiper will run along the stones before you, as if to show you the way to the best pools. (Bowing and teetering in the friendliest manner.)'

c. In the thick branches of the hemlocks that stretch across the stream, the tiny warblers chirp and twitter confidingly. (Dressed in their coats of many colors. Above your head.)

d. When the stream runs down through the pasture you will find the song sparrow singing happily. (Perched on his favorite limb of a young maple. Close beside the water. Through sunshine and through rain.)

e. While you are trying every fly in your book, the song sparrow will be chanting patience and encouragement. (Close above you. From a black gnat to a white miller. To entice the crafty old trout at the foot of the meadow-pool. For an hour at a time.)

f. And when success crowns your endeavor, and the particolored prize is glittering in your net, the bird breaks out in an ecstasy of congratulation. (At last. On the bough.)

Lesson XVIII - The Bras d'Or

The Bras d'Or is the most beautiful salt-water lake I have ever seen, and more beautiful than we had imagined a body of salt water could be. If the reader will take the map, he will see that two narrow estuaries, the Great and the Little Bras d'Or, enter the island of Cape Breton, on the ragged northeast coast, above the town of Sydney, and flow in, at length widening out and occupying the heart of the island. The water seeks out all the low places, and ramifies the interior, running away into lovely bays and lagoons, leaving slender tongues of land and picturesque islands, and bringing into the recesses of the land, to the remote country farms and settlements, the flavor of salt, and the fish and mollusks of the briny sea.

There is very little tide at any time, so that the shores are clean and sightly for the most part, like those of fresh-water lakes. It has all the pleasantness of a fresh-water lake, with all the advantages of a salt one. In the streams which run into it are the speckled trout, the shad, and the salmon; out of its depths are hooked the cod and the mackerel, and in its bays fattens the oyster.

This irregular lake is about a hundred miles long, if you measure it skillfully, and in some places ten miles broad; but so indented is it, that I am not sure but one would need, as we were informed, to ride a thousand miles to go round it, following all its incursions into the land. The hills about it are never more than five or six hundred feet high, but they are high enough for reposeful beauty, and offer everywhere reposeful lines.

From "Baddeck, and That Sort of Thing," by Charles Dudley Warner, Ch. III.

Study of the Model

Take your map, as Charles Dudley Warner directs, and follow point by point the description given. Notice how happy the writer is in his use of the words italicized in the following expressions: "the *ragged* northeast coast," "occupying the *heart* of the island," "out of its depths are *hooked* the cod and the mackerel," "in its bays *fattens* the oyster." Would he have made his picture of the lake so attractive if he had said *irregular* instead of *ragged*, *middle* instead of *heart*, *brought* instead of *hooked*, *grows* or *lives* instead of *fattens*?

Why is this description more attractive than many descriptions of lakes and other natural features, which you find in your geographies? For one reason, the writer had just seen for the first time this beautiful sheet of water, and the sight had filled him with delight and enthusiasm. It is generally easy to tell when one reads a composition whether or not its author liked his subject. A good rule in writing is to choose subjects that not merely interest you, but please you as well. Sometimes a subject is not pleasing to you for the reason that you know so little about it. After studying it you may find it pleasing enough to make it the subject of a composition.

Written Exercises

1. Outline the plan of the model.
2. If you live near a lake or a pond, so describe it as to make your readers wish to see it.
3. Bead in your geography a description of some lake.

Try to see the lake with your mind's eye, then write such a description of it as you might write after actually seeing it.

4. Rearrange the phrases and clauses of the following sentences wherever it is necessary to make the meaning clear.

Read again §§ 596 and 597 of Maxwell's "Advanced Lessons in English Grammar."

a. The lake was rippled with a breeze, and so it looked dull and sulky, though the sun shone like a child out of humor.

b. The water is strewn with islands, few of which are large enough to be inhabitable, in one portion.

c. There are two trees on the lawn between us and the lake, in front of our hotel, which we have taken to be yews.

d. There is a little hamlet of huts in a secluded dell that opens upon the most beautiful cove of the whole lake, inhabited by the people who are at work upon the railroad.

e. The trees overshadow it deeply, but there is some brilliant shrubbery which seems to light up the whole picture with a sweet and melancholy smile, on one side.

5. Explain the meanings of the following groups of synonyms. Follow the directions given for the similar exercise in Lesson VII.
Beautiful, fine, handsome, pretty.
Lovely, amiable, beloved.
Pleasant, agreeable, pleasing.
Clean, cleanly, pure.
Skillful, clever, expert, dexterous, adroit.

Lesson XIX - Little Johannes

It was warm by the pond, and still as death. The sun, flushed and tired from its day's work, seemed to be resting for a moment on the top of the distant ridge of dunes before diving below. Almost perfectly the smooth water reflected its glowing face. The overhanging leaves of the beech took advantage of the stillness to gaze intently at themselves in the mirror. The solitary heron, who was standing on one foot between the broad leaves of the water lilies, forgot that he had gone out to catch frogs, and stared in front of him, lost in thought.

Then Johannes came to the little grass plot to see the cloud grotto. Plump! plump! the frogs sprang from the shore. The mirror broke into ripples, the sun picture separated into broad stripes, and the beech leaves rustled crossly, for they had not looked at themselves sufficiently.

Fast bound to the naked roots of the beech lay a little old boat. Johannes had been strictly forbidden to get into it. Oh, how strong the temptation was this evening! Already the clouds were forming themselves into an awful gateway, behind which the sun would go to rest. Glittering little clouds ranged themselves in lines at the sides, like a bodyguard in golden armor. The surface of the water glowed also, and red sparks flew like arrows through the reeds.

Slowly Johannes unfastened the cord of the boat from the beech roots. To float there in the midst of that splendor! Presto, the dog, had already sprung into the boat, and, before his master had made up his mind, the reeds bent and pushed them both forward in the direction of the setting sun.

Translated from the Dutch of "De Kleine Johannes," by Frederik van Eeden.

Study of the Model

You have, of course, discovered that this model is incomplete. It is part of a long story in which many adventures of little Johannes are related. The reader feels when he comes to the end of this extract that the writer has stopped just as he was about to tell the most important and interesting thing in the story. The description of the quiet pond, of the warm evening, of the gorgeous sunset, and the account of the launching of the boat, were given to lead up to some exciting thing that happened to Johannes while he was on the water. In other words, all that is given here leads up to the main incident, or, as it is sometimes called, the climax.

In the original story a sprite, whom Johannes at first takes for a dragon fly, seats himself on the edge of the boat, and makes the acquaintance of the little boy. But there are a hundred other things that might have happened to Johannes as he took this forbidden boat ride. It will not be difficult for you to think of one of them.

Written Exercises

1. Finish the story by relating something that will be the main incident of the completed tale.
2. From the following hints begin stories, and finish them as you please. Imagine that you are telling these stories to children.

The Feast of St. Nicholas, by Jan Steen (c. 1665 – 1668)

a. Bess's mother, a poor widow, often went out to do a day's washing. At such times she would leave her little girl's dinner on a stand, so that she could get it as soon as she came home from school. One day, when Bess opened the door, she saw a chair upset, and her bread-and-milk bowl empty. What had happened during the mother's absence? What did Hess do?

b. A little country boy lost his way in the woods one day. He was met by a wild beast, but he escaped uninjured. How was he rescued?

Saved!

c. One day little Tom played with his ball in the parlor while his mother was out, and he broke a pretty vase. Two weeks later he surprised his mother by presenting her with a vase similar to the one he had broken. Where did he get it?

d. The only doll Betty had ever had was a corncob, with a piece of calico tied around it for a dress. The little girl used to play by herself in the woods near her father's house, where there was a hollow tree in which she kept her playthings. One time, on returning to her home after a long visit at her grandmother's, she hastened to her tree cupboard in order to get her doll and tell it all about the visit. To her surprise, she found, in place of the corncob, a beautiful wax doll. How had it come there?

3. The picture, The Feast of St. Nicholas, tells you as plainly as words could tell, the climax of a story. Invent a beginning for the story, and end it as the picture suggests. (In Holland children believe that St. Nicholas brings good things to good boys and girls, but fills the shoes of the naughty with coal.)

4. Write a story suggested by the picture entitled 'Saved!'.

Lesson XX - The Plot Against Odysseus

Then talked my crew among themselves, and said
That I had brought with me from Aeolus,
The large-souled son of Hippotas, rich gifts

Of gold and silver. Standing side by side
And looking at each other, thus they said:
"How wonderfully is our chief revered
And loved by all men, wander where he will
Into what realm soever! From the coast
Of Troy he sailed with many precious things,
His share of spoil, while we who with him went
And with him came, are empty-handed yet;
And now hath Aeolus, to show how much
He prizes him, bestowed the treasures here.
Come, let us see them; let us know how much
Of gold and silver is concealed in this."
Thus speaking to each other, they obeyed
The evil counsel. They untied the sack.
And straight the winds rushed forth and seized the ship.
And swept the crews, lamenting bitterly,
Far from their country out upon the deep.

Bryant's "Odyssey," Bk. X, ll. 43-62.

Study of the Model

Read the first sentence of the poem aloud. Now read this sentence: Then my crew talked among themselves, saying that I had brought with me rich gifts of gold and silver from Aeolus, the large-souled son of Hippotas. What is the difference in sound between the two sentences?

You can beat time for verse just as for a piece of music. Try it with the first line of this poem, and you will find that there are two syllables to every measure. To do this, emphasize these syllables: *talked — crew — mong — selves — said,* saying move lightly the syllable that should be where the dashes are.

We will measure off the line thus: —
<blockquote>Then talked | my crew | among | themselves | and said.</blockquote>

We see that we have five measures. These are called *feet.* Each of these feet has two syllables, a short foot and a long foot.

When a foot in poetry consists of two syllables, the first short and the second long, it is called an *iambic* foot.

Read the poems named in the following list, and notice that each is composed of iambic lines.

"Casabianca," Mrs. Hemans.
"Daybreak," Longfellow.
"The Parrot," Campbell.
"The Eagle," Tennyson.
"Lucy Gray," Wordsworth.
"John Gilpin," Cowper.
"Hohenlinden," Campbell.

Written Exercises

1. Mark off in measures, using bars and accents, the syllables in each line of the model.

2. Relate the incident narrated in the model, giving the words the usual order of prose. For an illustration of this, see the first paragraph of the *Study of the Model.*

3. In the same way relate the incidents narrated in the following selections from Bryant's translation of the "Odyssey."

"A Princess Washing Clothes," Bk. VI. ll. 94-124.
"The Lotus-eaters," Bk. IX, ll. 102-127.
"Circe's Palace," Bk. X, ll. 254-270.
"Circe's Spell," Bk. X, ll. 283-294.
"The Spell Broken," Bk. X, ll. 467-480.

4. Continue the following jingle, being careful to make each line consist of four iambic feet: —

An Animal Catalogue

The nimble mouse is small and gray;
He comes out when the cat's away.
The bright canary all day long
Delights the household with its song.
The pig has eyes quite small and dim, —
I trust you never act like him.
The lion is the forest king, etc.

Part II

Chapter One - Description

Lesson I - My Grandmother's Portrait

We have no family portraits, Prue and I; only a portrait of my grandmother hangs upon our parlor wall. It was taken nearly a century ago, and represents the venerable lady, whom I remember in my childhood in spectacles and comely cap, as a young and blooming girl.

She is sitting upon an old-fashioned sofa, by the side of a prim aunt of hers, and with her back to the open window. Her costume is quaint but handsome. It is a cream-colored dress made high in the throat, ruffled round the neck and over the bosom and shoulders, and the sleeves are tight, tighter than any of our coat sleeves, and also ruffled at the wrist. Around the plump and rosy neck hangs a necklace of large ebony beads. There are two curls upon the forehead, and the rest of the hair flows away in ringlets down the neck.

The hands hold an open book; the eyes look up from it with tranquil sweetness, and through the open window behind you see a quiet landscape — a hill, a tree, the glimpse of a river, and a few peaceful summer clouds.

Abridged from "Prue and I," by George William Curtis.

Study of the Model

Do you not find after reading the model that you can almost *see* the portrait? This shows that the description is a good one, — it is a picture made by means of language.

Observe how carefully the writer has set to work to cause you to see the picture as he sees it. First he tells whose portrait it is. Then, after stating where the girl is sitting, he begins to describe with great minuteness her costume. Why do you suppose so much space is given to the description of the costume?

In the last paragraph the eyes are described as *tranquil,* the landscape as *quiet,* and the clouds as *peaceful.* In what respect are the meanings of these three words similar? Can you tell from his use of these adjectives what impression the picture must have produced on the writer?

Following is an outline of the description: —
I. Introduction.
   1. Subject of portrait. 2. Date of portrait.
II. Detailed description.
   1. Posture. 2. Costume. 3. Necklace 4. Hair.
III. What the portrait suggests.
   1. Reading. 2. Peace and sweetness.

Simplicity

Cherry Ripe

Written Exercises

1. In your geography there are probably many pictures illustrating the peculiar costumes worn by the people of certain countries. Describe one of these so accurately that your classmates will be able to pick out the picture you have used.

2. Describe the costume of one of the members of your class. See whether your classmates can tell whose costume you have described.

3. In imitation of the model write descriptions of the pictures entitled 'Simplicity' and 'Cherry Ripe'.

4. Combine each of the following pairs of sentences into one simple sentence by making the second one of each pair a participial phrase. Observe that by doing this yon emphasize, in each case, the thought expressed by the first of the two sentences.

Example. My grandmother wears a cream-colored dress. It is made high in the throat.

My grandmother wears a cream-colored dress made high in the throat.

a. This is the picture of a dear little girl. She is dressed in a quaint costume.

b. The driver has a broad, full face. It is curiously mottled with red.

c. Like a cauliflower, he has a multiplicity of coats. The upper one reaches to his heels.

d. He wears about his neck a huge roll of colored handkerchief. This is knowingly knotted and tucked in at the bosom.

e. The slave wore a silver collar. It bore an inscription.

f. Sandals protected his feet. The sandals were bound with thongs made of boar's hide.

g. On one side of the warrior's saddle hung a short battle-ax. It was richly inlaid with Damascene carving.

h. Prince John rode at the head of his jovial party. He was splendidly dressed in crimson and gold.

Lesson II - The Imperial Library of Vienna

The hall is two hundred and forty-five feet long, with a magnificent dome in the center, under which stands the statue of Charles V, of Carrara marble surrounded by twelve other monarchs of the house of Hapsburg. The walls are of variegated marble richly ornamented with gold, and the ceiling and dome are covered with brilliant fresco-paintings. The library numbers three hundred thousand volumes and sixteen thousand manuscripts, which are kept in walnut cases gilded and adorned with medallions. The rich and harmonious effect of the whole cannot easily be imagined.

It is exceedingly appropriate that a hall of such splendor should be used to hold a library. The pomp of a palace may seem hollow and vain, for it is but the dwelling of a man; but no building can be too magnificent for the hundreds of great and immortal spirits to dwell in who have visited earth during thirty centuries.

From "Views A-Foot," by Bayard Taylor, Ch. XXII.

Study of the Model

Read the first sentence of the model. Imagine the writer standing where he can see the whole of this hall. Its great length is the first thing that strikes him, and then its magnificent dome with the thirteen statues beneath. He mentions these things first in his description because they were the first things that claimed his attention.

Read the second and third sentences. Why does the writer mention the walls and the paintings on ceiling and dome before mentioning the books and the bookcases? Is this model a description of the library or of the hall that contains the library? Read the whole of the first paragraph. What one word would you use to describe this hall?

Read the second paragraph. Observe that this is not a continuation of the description. The writer is no longer telling us what he sees. He is *thinking about* what he sees, and he gives us his thoughts or his *reflections.* Only the first part of this model, then, is a description.

Compare this model with that in the preceding lesson. Which of the two is the more purely descriptive?

Written Exercises

1. Make an outline of the model.
2. Write a description of a room in a public library you have visited, of your school library, or of any other room containing many books, with which you are acquainted. Imagine yourself standing where you can see the whole room, and describe only what you could see from that place. Write as though you were describing the room for some friend who has not seen it.
3. Write a description of the picture entitled 'Emerson's Library'.
4. Combine each of the following pairs of sentences into one complex sentence by making the second sentence of each pair a dependent clause. Use the phrases, *of which, under which, on which, between which,* etc.

Example. The hall has a magnificent dome in the center. A statue of Carrara marble stands under this dome.

The hall has a magnificent dome in the center, under which stands a statue of Carrara marble.

a. In the middle of Emerson's library is a round table. Several books, a portfolio, and a few smaller articles are on the table.

b. On one side of the room are two doors. An open fireplace is between these.

c. There are several pictures on the walls. The largest of these is a copy of Michelangelo's "The Three Fates."

d. One of the women in the picture holds a pair of shears. She is about to cut a long thread with them.

Lesson III - The Toyshop Window

Little Annie pulls me onward by the hand, till suddenly we pause at the most wondrous shop in all the town. Oh, my stars! Is this a toyshop, or is it fairyland? For here are gilded chariots, in which the king and queen of the fairies might ride side by side, while their courtiers, on these small horses, should gallop in triumphal procession before and behind the royal pair. Here, too, are dishes of chinaware, fit to be the dining set of those same princely personages, when they make a regal banquet in the stateliest hall of their palace, full five feet high, and behold their nobles feasting adown the long perspective of the table.

Here stands a turbaned Turk, threatening us with his saber, like an ugly heathen as he is. And next a Chinese mandarin, who nods his head at Annie and myself. Here we may review a whole army of horse and foot, in red and blue uniforms, with drums, fifes, trumpets, and all kinds of noiseless music; they have halted on the shelf of this window, after their weary march from Lilliput.

But what cares Annie for soldiers? No conquering queen is she, neither a Semiramis nor a Catharine; her whole heart is set upon that doll, who gazes at us with such a fashionable stare. Little Annie looks wishfully at the proud lady in the window. We will invite her home with us as we return. Meantime, good-by. Dame Doll. Oh, with your never-closing eyes, had you but an intellect to moralize on all that flits before them, what a wise doll would you be!

Abridged from "Little Annie's Ramble," by Nathaniel Hawthorne.

Study of the Model

You can tell by reading the first sentence of this model that it is part of a story; but by reading the rest you perceive that the part selected is really a *description* of a toyshop window. Who is describing the window, a child or a grown-up person?

Read the model carefully and tell what things the writer actually sees in the window and what he only imagines. For instance, he sees a tiny gilded chariot, and at once he imagines fairies riding in it. What does he imagine when he sees the small horses? the dishes of chinaware? the Turk? the toy soldiers?

In the last paragraph there is very little description. We are told that the doll has a fashionable stare, and that the eyes are never-closing. In the last sentence the writer does what he says the doll cannot do, — he *moralizes* on what he sees.

Compare this description with the two preceding descriptions. Do you see the toyshop window as plainly as yon see the young girl in her quaint costume, or as plainly as you see the splendid hall with its dome and its statues? If the description of the window had been given in order that you might know exactly how the toys were arranged, it would be a poor description. But it was given in order that you might know what delightful thoughts the sight of a toyshop window could suggest. Which of the three descriptions did you most enjoy reading?

Written Exercises

1. Make an outline of the model.
2. Write a description of the window or stand of a fruit store which you have carefully observed. Instead of saying merely that there were so many oranges here and so many lemons there, let your imagination help you to picture the places from which the fruits came, and make allusions to these places in your description. In describing a fruiterer's window, Charles Dickens speaks of "piles of filberts, mossy and brown, recalling in their fragrance ancient walks amongst the woods, and pleasant shufflings ankle deep through withered leaves." [1]
3. Imagine yourself standing before the window of a bakery, in company with a hungry child, for whom you are about to buy something to eat. Write a description of the window after the style of the model.
4. Change the following questions and exclamations to declarative sentences, and note how much less emphatic they become.

Examples. (1) But what cares Annie for soldiers?
But Annie does not care for soldiers.
(2) Oh, with your never-closing eyes, had you but an intellect to moralize on all that flits before them, what a wise doll would you be!
If, with your never-closing eyes, you had but an intellect to moralize on all that flits before them, you would be a very wise doll.

  a. Oh, my stars! Is this a toyshop, or is it fairyland?
  b. What a strange couple to go on their rambles together!
  c. How delightful to let the fancy revel on the dainties of a confectioner; those pies, with such white and flaky paste, their contents being a mystery; those dark, majestic masses, fit to be bridal loaves at the wedding of an heiress, mountains in size, their summits deeply snow-covered with sugar.
  d. Look! look at that great cloth spread out in the air, pictured all over with wild beasts, as if they had met together to choose a king, according to their custom in the days of Aesop.
  e. Mercy on us, what a noisy world we quiet people live in!

f. Sweet has been the charm of childhood on my spirit, throughout my ramble with little Annie!

g. Among all the town officers, chosen at March meeting where is he that sustains, for, a single year, the burden of such manifold duties as are in perpetuity, upon the Town Pump?

[1] From "A Christmas Carol," by Charles Dickens. School Comp.

Lesson IV – An Underground Flower

The stroller in the moist May woods will well remember those mauve-winged blooms among the moss that seem to flutter in the breeze, like a brood of tiny purple butterflies with fringy tails, or in a sheltered nook appear to have settled in a swarm among the wintergreen leaves. "False wintergreen" the plant is commonly called, its leaves bearing a slight resemblance to those of the aromatic checkerberry.

It is one of our oddest and prettiest spring flowers; in its very singular shape quite suggesting an orchid, with its two spreading petals and deep lavender-colored tasseled sleeve. But, indeed, it has long been laughing at us in that sleeve, as we have brought away its flowers from the woods, while we left its rarest and most important bloom behind us.

For the little *polygala* found out long ago that some means must be adopted to keep its foothold in the woods, so many were the eager hands that culled it every year. And so it formed a little plan to anchor itself in its home beyond the reach of bouquet hunters, offering one posy for the boutonnière, and another for mother earth — one playful flower for the world, another for serious use and posterity. But for this cunning resource I fear our pretty fringed *polygala* would have been exterminated in many of its haunts. Let us lose no time to seek the purple bloom in the woods, and gracefully acknowledge our humility. These pale, pouchlike underground flowers are not beautiful to look at, but they plant the mold with seeds every year, and thus perpetuate the purple beds of bloom.

From ""Sharp Eyes," by William Hamilton Gibson. Harper and Brothers.

Study of the Model

This model differs from the three preceding models in that it is a description not of a single thing but of a whole *class* of things. Instead of a description of a single specimen of this underground flower we have here a description of all the flowers of its kind. The writer does not give us such a description of the polygala as we should expect to find in a botany. His chief purpose in describing the plant is to draw attention to the pale pouchlike underground flowers that produce its seed; but in drawing our attention to these flowers; he tells us much besides about the appearance of the plant.

In order to enable another person to see with his mind's eye what we are describing, we frequently use comparisons. For instance, we say, "as black as coal," "as tall as you are," "the size of a silver dollar," etc. Notice the comparisons used in this model. Does it help you in forming a picture of the flowers to be told that they look "like a brood of tiny purple butterflies with fringy tails"? The writer of this description expected his readers to be persons who knew something about the appearance of checkerberries and orchids. If the readers knew nothing of checkerberries, would the comparison in the last sentence of the first paragraph be helpful? If they knew nothing of orchids, would the comparison in the first sentence of the second paragraph be helpful?

What is meant by the expression "to laugh in one's sleeve"? Did the flower really laugh? Did it really "form a little plan to anchor itself in its home"? Does it really "offer" its posies? Do you enjoy the description all the more on account of this fanciful and humorous way of putting things?

Written Exercises

1. Make an outline of the model.

2. In imitation of the model describe and illustrate one of the peculiar plants mentioned in the following list, or some other that you have observed or read about.

SARRACENIA PURPUREA, THE PITCHER PLANT OF THE NORTHERN UNITED STATES.

DIONÆA, THE VENUS'S FLY-TRAP.

SKUNK CABBAGE.

PAINTED-CUP.

a. Pitcher plant.

Leaves form pitchers that hold water in which insects are drowned.

b. Venus's fly-trap.

Leaves have little spines on margins and upper surface, and they instantly close over insects and other objects which light upon them.

CLOSED GENTIAN.   POISON IVY.

c. Skunk cabbage.

Flower comes in early spring before the leaves; belongs to the same family as the calla.

d. Painted-cup.

Flowers so insignificant as to be seldom observed, but surrounded by gorgeous scarlet-tipped leaves.

e. Closed gentian.

Flowers never open.

f. Poison ivy.

> "Berries red,
> Have no dread!
> Berries white,
> Poisonous sight!
> Leaves three.
> Quickly flee!"

3. Describe minutely the leaves of a plant designated by your teacher. Describe the form, the arrangement on the stem, the margin, the apex, the base, and, if they have any, the petiole and the stipules.

4. Combine each of the following groups of sentences into one compound sentence. Choose your conjunctions [1] so carefully that they will show the exact relations between the members of the sentences.

Example. Those pale pouchlike underground flowers are not good to look at. They plant the mold with seeds every year. Thus they perpetuate the purple beds of bloom.

Those pale pouchlike underground flowers are not good to look at, but they plant the mold with seeds every year, and thus perpetuate the purple beds of bloom.

a. We have all heard of four-leaved, five-leaved, and manyleaved clovers. It is, perhaps, not generally known that many of the clover tribe start out in life as one-leaved clovers.
b. Smilacina differs from Solomon's seal in many respects. One is often mistaken for the other.
c. The crocus comes up in the early spring. We may conclude that it has an underground stem.
d. The potato grows underground. It is often mistaken for a root.
e. The orange tree is a native of warm climates. It is sometimes cultivated in hot-houses in the North.
f. The skunk cabbage has neither beauty nor fragrance. On account of its early blooming it has many admirers.
g. Flax has a pretty blue flower. Hemp has a sad-colored blossom.

[1] See Maxwell's "Advanced Lessons in English Grammar," § 462, for a list of the coordinate conjunctions.

Chapter Two - Narration

Lesson V - The Owl in the Cherry Tree

The great bugaboo of the birds is the owl. The owl snatches them from off their roosts at night, and gobbles up their young in their nests. He is a veritable ogre to them, and his presence fills them with consternation and alarm.

One season, to protect my early cherries, I placed a large stuffed owl amid the branches of the tree. Such a racket as there instantly began about my grounds is not pleasant to think upon! The orioles and robins fairly "shrieked out their affright." The news instantly spread in every direction, and apparently every bird in town came to see that owl in the cherry-tree, and every bird took a cherry, so that I lost more fruit than if I had left the owl in-doors. With craning necks and horrified looks the birds alighted upon the branches, and between their screams would snatch off a cherry, as if the act was some relief to their outraged feelings.

From "Birds and Bees," by John Burroughs.

Study of the Model

Notice the difference between the two paragraphs of this selection. The first makes a statement concerning the way in which some birds regard the owl.

The second tells a short story or anecdote which illustrates this statement. The writer of a good anecdote has in mind one point which he brings out briefly and forcibly in his story.

This anecdote is particularly enjoyable on account of its humor. The writer makes us know that he enjoyed the joke although it was at his own expense. It is because he wishes us to see the humorous side of the incident that he uses some exaggerations. Do you believe that the news *instantly* spread in every direction? Did the birds really have *horrified looks*? What other exaggerations do you find?

Written Exercises

1. Write an anecdote to illustrate a dog's faithfulness; a horse's good sense; an eagle's power of vision; a monkey's imitativeness; a lion's strength; an elephant's docility; a beaver's ingenuity; a mule's stubbornness; the industry of bees; or the patience of the ox.

2. From the following hints write an anecdote to illustrate some trait of an animal. State what trait the anecdote illustrates.

a. A horse is stolen from a farmer. Later he sees it being ridden by another man, and, with the assistance of the people standing near, he makes the thief dismount; whereupon the horse goes directly to the farmer's stable.

b. One dark night a horse, drawing his master in a carriage, comes to a bridge which he cannot be induced to cross. The master learns from the tollgate keeper that the bridge is broken in the middle.

c. A certain hen lays an egg each day. Its owner, not being satisfied, increases the quantity of its food, and the hen gives up laying altogether.

3. Write an anecdote of an animal, using one of the following as an introduction.

a. The gray squirrel even when caged does not lose its habit of laying up a store of food for winter use.

b. "A cow can bid her calf, by secret signal, probably of the eye, to run away, or to lie down and hide itself." (Emerson.)

c. A mole, like the lad in the fairy tale, who could not learn how to shiver and shake, does not know what fear is.

d. To many animals the sense of smell is of more importance than the sense of sight or of hearing.

e. It is difficult to ascertain what the tastes of the ostrich may be while it is roaming the desert, but when in captivity no other animal shows less nicety in the choice of its food.

f. The deer kind are remarkable for the arts they employ in order to deceive the dogs.

g. The fox has, in all ages, been celebrated for craftiness.

4. Combine each of the following groups of sentences into one sentence — simple, complex, or compound — being careful to use the form that express-

es most clearly and briefly what you consider to be the relations existing between the given sentences.

Example. One dark night a horse was drawing his master in a carriage. He came to a bridge. He could not be induced to cross it.

One dark night a horse, drawing his master in a carriage, came to a bridge which he could not be induced to cross.

a. A sea urchin has legs all around his body. It really does not matter whether he walks upright, on his side, or upside down.

b. A number of nests have been found upon rocks behind cascades. Here they were kept wet by spray from the falling water.

c. Many animals have lairs and dens and nests underground. In these they rest and bring up their little ones.

d. The mole has a subterranean dwelling place. He does not confine himself to it. He goes rambling off in any direction he chooses in the solid earth, almost as a fish swims in water.

e. The prairie dog does not look like a dog. He does not act as a dog acts. He does not eat what a dog eats.

f. Like the bees, the ants have what are called their queens. The so-called queens possess no power to command their subjects.

Lesson VI - Gluck and the Little Old Gentleman

"Hollo!" said the little gentleman, "that's not the way to answer the door; I'm wet, let me in."

"I beg pardon, sir," said Gluck, "I'm very sorry, but I really can't."

"Can't what?" said the old gentleman.

"I can't let you in, sir, — I can't, indeed; my brothers would beat me to death, sir, if I thought of such a thing. What do you want, sir?"

"Want?" said the old gentleman, petulantly, "I want fire and shelter; and there's your great fire there blazing, crackling, and dancing on the walls, with nobody to feel it. Let me in, I say; I only want to warm myself."

"He does look very wet," said little Gluck to himself; "I'll just let him in for a quarter of an hour." Round he went to the door, and opened it; and as the little gentleman walked in, through the house came a gust of wind that made the old chimneys totter.

"That's a good boy," said the little gentleman. "Never mind your brothers. I'll talk to them."

"Pray, sir, don't do any such thing," said Gluck. "I can't let you stay till they come; they'd be the death of me."

"Dear me," said the old gentleman, "I'm very sorry to hear that. How long may I stay?"

"Only till the mutton's done, sir," replied Gluck, "and it's very brown."

Adapted from "The King of the Golden River," by John Ruskin.

Study of the Model

You remember, perhaps, how the story "Alice in Wonderland" commences. "Alice was beginning to get very tired of sitting by her sister on the bank, and of having nothing to do: once or twice she had peeped into the book her sister was reading, but it had no pictures or conversations in it, 'and what is the use of a book,' thought Alice, 'without pictures or conversations?'" Do you not share Alice's liking for conversations in stories?

From a conversation or dialogue that is well written we can usually learn something about the characters of the persons who are talking. From a reading of the model you can answer these questions: What words of the old gentleman show that he was not very meek and humble? How do you know that he was not ill-natured? How do you know that Gluck was well-bred? kind-hearted? timid?

In inventing a conversation, determine first what kind of persons shall do the talking, and then see to it that they say nothing which it would not be natural for such persons to say. Although you should not let your characters talk in a stiff, goody-goody way, yet you should make their language more correct than the ordinary speech of real conversations. Do not let your imaginary persons make long speeches.

Written Exercises

1. Write an imaginary conversation that took place, —

    a. Between a teacher and a pupil who frequently comes late to school.

    b. Between a mother and her little daughter who wants to play before she has studied her lessons.

    c. Between two boys, each of whom claims that he has won a certain game.

    d. Between two boys, the older of whom is conducting the younger through a menagerie.

    e. Between a city girl and a country girl, one of whom is showing the other some of the interesting sights of the city or the country.

2. Write the dialogue that may have taken place between the little girl and the doge (duke) mentioned in the following description of a picture.

"It represents some scene from the history of Venice. On an open piazza a noble prisoner, wasted and pale from long confinement, has just had an interview with his children. He reaches his arm toward them as if for the last time, while a savage keeper drags him away. A lovely little girl kneels at the feet of the doge, but there is no compassion in his stern features, and it is easy to see that her father is doomed."

From "Views A-Foot," by Bayard Taylor.

3. Tell all you can about the persons taking part in the following dialogues.

"You must be a stranger, sir, in these parts."

"Yes; my home is very far from here." "How far?"
"More than a thousand leagues." ...
"More than a thousand leagues! And why have you come so far from home?"
"To travel, to see how you live in this country."
"Have you no relations in your own?"
"Yes, I have both brothers and sisters, a father and —"
"And a mother?"
"Thank Heaven, I have."
"And did you leave *her*?"

From "Outre-mer," by H. W. Longfellow.

"Shut your eyes, Maggie."
"What for?"
"You never mind what for. Shut 'em when I tell you. Now which'll you have, Maggie — right hand or left?"
"I'll have that with the jam run out," said Maggie.
"Why, you don't like that. You may have it if it comes to you fair, but I shan't give it you without. Right hand or left — you choose, now. Ha a a! You keep your eyes shut, now, else you shan't have any."
"Left hand," said Maggie.
"You've got it," said Tom, in rather a bitter tone.
"What! the bit with the jam run out?"
"No; here, take it."
"Oh, please, Tom, have it; I don't mind — I like the other: please take this."
"No, I shan't."
After Maggie had eaten her half of the puff, Tom said, "Oh, you greedy thing!"
"Oh, Tom, why didn't you ask me?"
"*I* wasn't going to ask you for a bit. You might have thought of it without, when you knew I gave you the best bit."
"But I wanted you to have it — you know I did."
"Yes, but I wasn't going to do what wasn't fair, like Spouncer. He always takes the best bit, if you don't punch him for it; and if you choose the best with your eyes shut, he changes his hands. But if I go halves, I'll go 'em fair — only I wouldn't be a greedy."

Adapted from "The Mill on the Floss," by George Eliot, Ch. VI.

4. Write the dialogue that might have taken place between the two persons in either of the pictures entitled The Apple Parer, and Always Tell the Truth.

5. Rewrite the following anecdotes, using the direct instead of the indirect form of reporting what was said by any one. Note the increase in clearness and emphasis. Be careful to use quotation marks properly, and to begin the quoted sayings with capitals.

Example. One morning Washington's secretary having come late found Washington waiting for him. He tried to excu.se himself by explaining that his watch was slow, but Washington replied that either the secretary must get another watch or he should have to get another secretary.

The Apple Parer

Always Tell the Truth

One morning Washington's secretary having come late found Washington waiting for him. "My watch is slow," he said, trying to excuse himself. Washington replied, "Either you must get another watch, or I shall have to get another secretary."

a. An artist had two pets, a cat and a kitten. One day a friend of his, having noticed two holes in the artist's door, one large and the other small, asked what they were for. The artist informed him that they were there to let the two pets in and out. The friend asked why there should be two holes when one would do as well. The painter called him a stupid fellow and asked him how he supposed the big cat could go through the little hole. When the friend said that the little cat could go through the big hole, the artist laughed and confessed that he had never thought of that.

b. John offered to prove to his father that the two pigeons on the supper-table were three. When the father asked how he could do this, John replied that the first pigeon was one, the other was two, and that one and two make three. To this the father quickly responded that the mother might take the first pigeon, he would take the second, and John might have the third.

c. At the battle of Crécy the Prince of Wales was so hard pressed that the Earl of Warwick sent a message to the king beseeching him to send aid to his son, The king, who was overlooking the battle from a windmill, asked whether the prince was dead. The messenger replied that he was not. The king asked whether he was wounded, and the messenger said no. Then the king asked whether he had been thrown to the ground. The messenger said no, but that he was hard pressed. Then the king bade the messenger go back to those who had sent him and tell them that he should give no aid, as he had set his heart upon his son's proving himself a brave knight to whom the honor of a great victory should belong.

Lesson VII - The Teapot

There was a proud Teapot, proud of being porcelain, proud of its long spout, proud of its broad handle; it had something before and behind; the spout before, the handle behind, and that was what it talked about. It did not talk of its lid, — that was cracked, it was riveted, it had faults, — and one does not talk about one's faults, there are plenty of others to do that. The cups, the cream pot, and sugar bowl, the whole tea service would be reminded much more of the lid's weakness and talk about that, than of the sound handle and the remarkable spout. The Teapot knew it.

It stood on the table that was spread for tea, it was lifted by a very delicate hand: but the very delicate hand was awkward, the Teapot fell, the spout snapped off, the handle snapped off, the lid was no worse to speak of — the worst had been spoken of that. The Teapot lay in a swoon on the floor, while the boiling water ran out of it. It was a horrid shame, but the worst was that they jeered at it; they jeered at it, and not at the awkward hand.

"I shall never lose the memory of that!" said the Teapot, when it afterward talked to itself of the course of its life. "I was called an invalid, and placed in a corner, and the day after was given away to a woman who begged victuals. I fell into poverty, and stood dumb both outside and in, but there, as I stood, began my better life. One is one thing and becomes quite another. Earth was placed in me: for a Teapot, that is the same as being buried, but in the earth was placed a flower bulb. Who placed it there, who gave it, I know not; given it was, and it took the place of the Chinese leaves and the boiling water, the broken 4iandle and spout. And the bulb lay in the earth, the bulb lay in me, it became my heart, my living heart, such as I never before had. There was life in me, power and might: my pulses beat, the bulb put forth sprouts, it was the springing up of thoughts and feelings: they burst forth in flower. I saw it, I bore it, I forgot myself in its delight. Blessed it is to forget one's self in another. The bulb gave me no thanks, it did not think of me — it was admired and praised. I was so glad at that; how happy must it have been! One day I heard it said that it ought to have a better pot. I was thumped on my back — that was rather hard to bear; but the flower was put in a better pot — and I was thrown away in the yard where I lie as an old crock; but I have the memory: that I can never lose."

Abridged from "The Teapot," by Haus Christian Andersen.

Study of the Model

The first fairy tales that Hans Andersen wrote out were reproductions of folk stories he had heard as a child. After inventing a few similar tales, he began to write the kind for which he became famous throughout the world. In. these he *personified* dumb creatures and things without life; that is, he made ducks, storks, and beetles, flowers and trees, and the ordinary objects that a child sees every day about the house, talk and act like human beings. He did not, like Aesop, tell his stories to teach a lesson; he told them to entertain children, and it is natural for children to personify their playthings. The homelier and more commonplace the object that Andersen personified, the more delightful he seemed to make the story about it. Thorwaldsen, the great sculptor, said to him once, "Come now, write us a new and comical story. I wonder if you could make one up about the darning-needle!" And Andersen set to work and wrote his well-known tale called "The Darning Needle."

The model is a story of this kind. Notice that the Teapot has an individuality all its own. It has the natural feelings of a real person, being, in the beginning, proud of its good looks, ashamed of its weakness, sensitive to ridicule, indignant at being treated unjustly; and later becoming softened and ennobled by suffering.

Other stories of this kind by Hans Andersen are: —

"The Silver Shilling."   "The Buckwheat."
"The Shirt Collar."   "The Toad."
"The Old Street Lamp."   "The Snowdrop."
"The Pen and Inkstand."   "The Snow Man."
"The Windmill."   "Five out of one Shell."
"The Fir Tree."   "There is a Difference."
"The Flax."

Written Exercises

1. Make an outline of the model.
2. Write a story in imitation of the model. The following suggestions may be helpful.

a. The Cup.

It was proud of its gilt band. It belonged to Baby, who one day broke off its handle. It was then given to a poor little invalid, who placed a fresh rose in it, and afterward kept in it dried rose leaves.

b. The Salt Shaker.

It was made of cut glass, and it had a silver top. After it was broken it was filled with water and put into a canary's cage.

c. The Doll.

It had come from Paris, and it was proud of its pretty face and its satin dress. One day its mistress left it out in the sun. Its beauty was destroyed. Then it was given to a poor girl who dressed it in plain muslin.

d. The Tablecloth.

Because it had a drawn-work border it was used only on state occasions. One day a guest accidentally made a great rent in the border. After this the cloth was torn into strips and used for bandages in a hospital.

3. Rearrange the words of the following sentences so that they stand in the usual order (the complete subject before the predicate), and note the difference in force.

Example. Who placed it there, who gave it, I know not.
I do not know who placed it there or who gave it.

a. All around the fields and meadows were great woods, and in the midst of these woods deep lakes.

b. Into the water the Ugly Duckling shall go, even if I have to push him in.

c. In a corner formed by two houses, one of which was a little farther from the street than the other, the little match girl sat down.

d. Down came the storm.

e. "Under a spreading chestnut tree
   The village smithy stands."

f. "Black were her eyes as the berry that grows on the thorn by the wayside."

g. "Bent but not broken by age was the form of the notary public."

h. Four times the sun had risen and set.

i. Swift of foot was Hiawatha.

Lesson VIII - The Death of Wolfe

The order was given to charge. Then over the field rose the British cheer, mixed with the fierce yell of the Highland slogan. Some of the corps pushed forward with the bayonet; some advanced firing. The clansmen drew their broadswords and dashed on, keen and swift as bloodhounds.

At the English right, though the attacking column was broken to pieces, a fire was still kept up, chiefly, it seems, by sharpshooters from the bushes and cornfields, where they had lain for an hour or more. Here Wolfe himself led the charge, at the head of his Louisville grenadiers. A shot shattered his wrist. He wrapped his handkerchief about it and kept on. Another shot struck him, and he still advanced, when a third lodged in his breast. He staggered, and sat on the ground. Lieutenant Brown of the grenadiers, one Henderson, a volunteer in the same company, and a private soldier, aided by an officer of artillery who ran to join them, carried him in their arms to the rear. He begged them to lay him down. They did so, and asked if he would have a surgeon. "There's no need," he answered: "it's all over with me." A moment after, one of them cried out, "They run; see how they run!" "Who run?" Wolfe demanded, like a man roused from sleep. "The enemy, sir. Egad, they give way everywhere!" "Go, one of you, to Colonel Burton," returned the dying man; "tell him to march Webb's regiment down to Charles River, to cut off their retreat from the bridge." Then, turning on his side, he murmured, "Now, God be praised, I will die in peace!" and in a few moments his gallant soul had fled.

From Parkman's "Montcalm and Wolfe." Little, Brown, & Company.

Study of the Model

In writing historical narratives it is of the first importance that we tell the truth. It is not always easy to find out the truth about actual events, but a real historian spares no pains in searching for it. It was said of a certain historian, "he reads twenty books to write a sentence; he travels a hundred miles to make a line of description."

We may, however, know the facts in regard to a particular historical event, but perhaps we have no power to put ourselves in the place of those taking part in it, and so we fail to realize the event. Or, perhaps, we can ourselves see with the mind's eye just how the thing happened, but we have no power to make others see.

To write an historical narrative, then, we must do three things; namely, —
1. Study, in order to learn all the facts of the case.
2. Put ourselves in the places of the actors.
3. So tell the story as to make the event seem as real to the reader as it seems to us.

Written Exercises

1. Read two or more accounts of one of the events mentioned in the following lists, try to imagine just how the event occurred, and then write your own account of it.
   a. Braddock's Defeat.
   b. The Death of Nathan Hale.
   c. Allen's Capture of Ticonderoga.
   d. Capture of Stony Point by "Mad Anthony Wayne."

e. The Fight between the *Bon Homme Richard* and the *Serapis*.
f. The Fight between the *Constitution* and the *Guerrière*.
g. The Fight between the *Merrimac* and the *Monitor*.
h. Perry's Victory on Lake Erie.
i. The Battle of Tippecanoe.
j. The Battle of New Orleans.
k. The Battle of Gettysburg.
l. Sherman's March to the Sea.
m. Sheridan's Ride.

2. By placing them out of their usual order, emphasize those words in the following sentences, which, in your opinion, ought to be emphasized. [1]

Example. The British cheer then rose over the field.
Then over the field rose the British cheer.
a. That famous battle was thus fought.
b. The greatest battle that the sun had ever looked on then began.
c. A council of Athenian officers was summoned two thousand three hundred and forty years ago, on the slope of one of the mountains that look over the plain of Marathon.
d. The little army, chanting the hymn of battle, bore down upon the host of the foe.
e. The Greeks came on.
f. Miltiades brought his men on at a ran instead of advancing at the usual slow pace of the phalanx.
g. The six hundred rode into the jaws of death.

[1] See Maxwell's "Advanced Lessons in English Grammar," §§ 593-597.

Chapter Three - Exposition

Lesson IX - Dogwatches

The crew are divided into two divisions, as equally as may be, called the watches. Of these, the chief mate commands the larboard, and the second mate the starboard. They divide the time between them, being on and off duty, or, as it is called, on deck and below, every other four hours.

An explanation of the "dogwatches" may, perhaps, be necessary to one who has never been at sea. Their purpose is to shift the watches each night, so that the same watch shall not be on deck at the same hours throughout a voyage. In order to effect this, the watch from four to eight p.m. is divided iiito two half watches, one from four to six, and the other from six to eight. By this means they divide the twenty-four hours into seven watches instead of six, and thus shift the hours every night. As the dogwatches come during twilight, after the day's work is done, and before the night watch is set, they are the watches in which everybody is on deck. The captain is up, walking on the weather side of the quarterdeck, the chief mate on the lee side, and the second mate about the weather gangway. The steward has finished his work in the cabin, and has come up to smoke his pipe with the cook in the galley. The crew are sitting on the windlass or lying on the forecastle, smoking, singing, or telling long yarns. At eight o'clock eight bells are struck, the log is hove, the watch set, the wheel relieved, the galley shut up, and the watch off duty goes below.

From "Two Years Before the Mast," by Richard Henry Dana, Jr., Ch. III.

Study of the Model

This model neither describes the appearance of certain sailors who form a watch on board a ship, nor does it tell a story about a particular watch. It explains what "dogwatches" are, and how the duties of such watches are performed. The model is, therefore, neither a description nor a narrative, it is an explanation or an exposition.

Since the purpose of an explanation is to make readers understand the thing explained, it is important that a plan be made and then carefully followed. The plan of this model might be expressed as follows: —

I. Watches in general.
 1. Their purpose.
 2. Their duties.
II. Dogwatches.
 1. What their purpose is.
 2. How this purpose is accomplished.
 3. What the occupations of officers and crew are.

Written Exercises

1. Write the model from memory, using the outline given above.
2. In imitation of the model, write an outline for an explanation of one of the following: —
 a. School monitors.
 b. A baseball nine.
 c. A football team.
 d. The three kinds of bees in a hive.
 e. The officers of a society or club.
 f. How the United States Senate is kept a permanent body.
 g. How the President of the United States is elected.
 h. How a patent is obtained.
 i. How outlines are made and compositions are written and corrected.
3. Write a composition from your outline.
4. Use in original sentences or explain the meanings of the following words, which you will find in *Dogwatches.*

Example. The *galley* is the cooking room on board ship.

crew   weather   gangway   chief mate   quarter-deck   second mate   cabin   steward   forecastle   larboard   windlass   starboard   log   weather side   yarns   lee side   deck   explanation   captain

Lesson X - The Camp Fire

In the making of fires there is as much difference as in the building of houses. Everything depends upon the purpose that you have in view. There is the camp fire, and the cooking fire, and the smudge fire, and the little friendship fire, — not to speak of other minor varieties. Each of these has its own proper style of architecture, and to mix them is false art and poor economy.

The object of the camp fire is to give heat, and incidentally light, to your tent or shanty. You can hardly build this kind of a fire unless you have a good ax and know how to chop. For the first thing that you need is a solid backlog, the thicker the better, to hold the heat and reflect it into the tent. This log must not be too dry, or it will burn out quickly. Neither must it be too damp, else it will smolder and discourage the fire. The best wood for it is the body of a yellow birch, and next to that, a green balsam. It should be five or six feet long, and at least two and a half feet in diameter. If you cannot find a tree thick enough, cut two or three lengths of a smaller one; lay the thickest log on the ground first, about ten or twelve feet in front of the tent; drive two strong stakes behind it, slanting a little backward; and lay the other logs on top of the first, resting against the stakes.

Now you are ready for the hand-chunks, or andirons. These are shorter sticks of wood, eight or ten inches thick, laid at right angles to the backlog, four or five feet apart. Across these you are to build up the firewood proper.

If you like a fire to blaze up at first with a splendid flame, and then burn on with an enduring heat far into the night, a young white birch with the bark on is the tree to choose. Six or eight round sticks of this laid across the hand-chunks, with perhaps a few quarterings of a larger tree, will make a glorious fire.

But before you put these on, you must be ready to light up. A few splinters of dry spruce or pine or balsam, stood endwise against the backlog, or, better still, piled up in a pyramid between the hand-chunks; a few strips of birch bark; and one good match, — these are all that you want.

In the woods, the old-fashioned brimstone match of our grandfathers — the match with a brown head and a stout stick and a dreadful smell — is the best. But if you have only one, you would better not trust even that to light your fire directly Use it first to touch off a roll of birch bark which you hold in your hand. Then, when the bark is well alight, crinkling and curling, push it under the heap of kindlings, give the flame time to take a good hold, and lay your wood over it, a stick at a time, until the whole pile is blazing. Now your fire is started. Your friendly little gnome with the red hair is ready to serve you through the night.

Abridged from "Fisherman's Luck," by Henry Van Dyke, Ch. XI.

Study of the Model

This model neither describes the appearance of a camp fire, nor tells a story about one; it explains what camp fires are for, and how they are built. It is therefore not a description nor a narrative, it is an explanation or exposition.

The plan of this model is easy to discover. We are told in the beginning that there are many kinds of fires and that each has its own proper style of architecture. Then is given the purpose of the camp fire. After that begins the explanation of the way in which the fire is built.

In making this explanation the writer must have imagined himself actually building a fire, for the order of the explanation follows the order of building — the backlog, the hand-chunks, and the firewood proper are obtained and laid in place, and then comes the lighting up. The reason why the explanation is so easy to understand and so easy to remember, notwithstanding its length, is that the plan is sensible and is carefully worked out. When you have an exposition well planned you have done the hardest part of the work.

Written Exercises

1. Make an outline of the model.
2. Write the model from memory, using your outline.
3. In imitation of the model, write an outline of an explanation of one of the following: —
a. The kitchen fire. *b.* The bonfire. *c.* The smudge fire. *d.* The friendship fire. *e.* The blacksmith's fire.
4. Write a composition from your outline.
5. Use in original sentences or explain the meanings of the following expressions, which you will find in *The Camp Fire.*

minor varieties   enduring heat
style of architecture   glorious fire
false art   dreadful smell
poor economy   touch off
shanty   crinkling and curling bark
smolder   kindlings
discourage the fire   andirons
splendid flame   friendly little gnome

Lesson XI - The First Mail in America

The first mail on the American continent started from New York for Boston on New Year's Day, 1673. The postman followed the Bowery Lane till it merged into the wagon road just finished to the new village of Harlem. After a cooling draught he was ready to go on his way past "Annie's Hook," or Pelham Manor, to Greenwich and Stamford, and so on to New Haven, Hartford, and Springfield, crossing all rivers and arms of the sea in boats, as was necessary until the last years of the eighteenth century. Now it was a stretch of newly built English wagon road that our postman followed, but oftener a mere bridle path, or an ancient Indian trail, and sometimes the way must needs be indicated by marking trees in the virgin forest. From Springfield eastward his path must have followed the same winding water courses of which the Boston and Albany Railroad now takes advantage, climbing near Quabaug (Brookfield) to a thousand feet above sea level, then gently descending into the pleasant valley of the Charles.

While our indefatigable carrier was thus earning his "handsome livelihood," a locked box stood in the secretary's office in New York awaiting his return, and in it from day to day the little heap of eastward bound letters grew. When the postman returned with his prepaid mail he emptied his New York bag on a broad table in the coffee-house where citizens most did congregate. That locked box and that coffee-house table had in them the prophecy of the great post-office that now stands in City Hall Park, and indirectly of all the post offices, urban and rural, in English-speaking America.

Abridged from "The Dutch and Quaker Colonies in America," by John Fiske, Vol. II, Ch. X.

Study of the Model

This explanation of the way in which letters were carried between New York and Boston in 1673 is interesting because it reads like a story. By narrating the doings of one particular postman, the writer of this selection really gives an explanation of the mail service of those early days. Other examples of this kind of explanation we have studied in Lessons XIII and XVII (Part I).

Written Exercises

1. Make an outline of the model.
2. Write the model from memory, using your outline.
3. In imitation of the model, write an explanation of one of the following: —

a. The first telegraph line in America.

b. The first passenger railway in America.

c. The overland route to California in 1849.

d. The mail service of to-day.

e. The letter-carrier of to-day.

f. A journey up the Hudson in 1807.

g. How cotton was raised before the invention of the cotton gin.

h. Traveling by the Erie Canal.

4. Change the following sentences by denying the opposite of what is said. Notice whether these changes make the sentences more emphatic or less so.

Example. In 1673 it was a difficult matter to carry the mail from New York to Boston.

In 1673 it was no easy matter to carry the mail from New York to Boston.

At Hartford the postman made his first change of horses.

The postman did not change horses until he reached Hartford.

a. In 1760 there were but eight mails a year from Philadelphia to the Potomac River.

6. When postal affairs were placed in the capable hands of Benjamin Franklin there were, for the first time, regular and trustworthy mails.

c. A century ago every farmer's daughter knew how to weave and to spin.

d. Before the invention of the cotton-gin a man could clean only a pound of cotton a day.

e. Four-wheeled wagons were but little used in New England until after the war of 1812.

f. The Erie Canal, first proposed to the New York legislature in 1768, was completed in 1825.

g. The history of whale-fishing in New England is the history of one of the most fascinating industries the world has ever known.

h. The kitchen in the farmhouses of the colonies was the most cheerful, homelike, and picturesque room in the house.

Lesson XII - Millet's "Feeding Her Chickens"

In the "Woman Feeding Her Chickens," I have tried to give the idea of a nest of birds being fed by their mother.

From "Jean Francois Millet: His Life and Letters," by Julia Cartwright, Part III, Ch. XI.

Feeding her Chickens

Landseer's "The Highland Shepherd's Chief Mourner"

The dog's breast is pressed close against the wood of the coffin. The convulsive clinging of the paws has dragged the blanket off the trestle, and the head is laid, close and motionless, upon its folds. The fall of the eye is fixed and tearful in its utter hopelessness. The rigidity of repose marks that there has been no motion nor change in the trance of agony since the last blow was struck on the coffin-lid. Quietness and gloom fill the chamber. The spectacles marking the place where the Bible was last closed, indicate how lonely has been the life, how unwatched the departure, of him who is now laid solitary in his last sleep.

Adapted from "Modern Painters," by John Ruskin, Vol. I, Ch. II.

Study of the Models

When you have a thought that you wish to share with another person, you express your thought in words. If you were an artist, you would express some of your thoughts in another kind of language—the language of pictures. Millet did not paint the picture called "Feeding Her Chickens" just because he happened to see a real scene like this, and knew it would make a pretty picture. His thought was, "Mothers and fathers, whether they are human beings or only the so-called lower animals, work hard in order that their children may be cared for"; and he expressed this thought, not in the commonplace words just quoted, but in a beautiful picture.

The First Step

It is interesting when looking at a picture to try to learn from it the thought the artist wished to convey. This is what is called interpreting the picture, or explaining its meaning. It is not the same as merely describing the appearance of the picture, as is done in Lesson X, Part One. Sometimes, however, in describing a picture we also explain it. "The Highland Shepherd's Chief Mourner" was painted by Landseer, the celebrated painter of animals. Read Ruskin's explanation of the picture. How does Landseer show that the dog was a real *mourner*? How does he show that the dog was the shepherd's *chief* mourner?

The Shepherd's Bible

It has been said that "the greatest picture is that which conveys to the mind of the spectator the greatest number of the greatest ideas." [1]

According to this theory which of the pictures – The First Step, or, The Shepherd's Bible - is, in your opinion, the greater? Why do you think so?

Written Exercises

1. What thought does Millet express in his picture called "The First Step"? (Does it suggest to your mind a scene from bird life?)
2. Write an explanation or interpretation of Landseer's "The Shepherd's Bible." (Suppose a person younger than yourself has asked you to tell why the hat and the book are lying on the stone, what the dogs are waiting for, etc.)
3. Write a *description* of any one of the four pictures given in this lesson. Begin by describing the principal figure or group of figures — that which gives meaning to the picture.
4. Bring to school, or find in your reader or on the walls of your schoolroom, a picture which, in your opinion, expresses a great thought. Write an explanation of the picture.
5. Read the following descriptions of pictures. Give an explanation of each picture or tell what thought each expresses.

a. A barefooted boy is seated on the stump of a tree, crying. Before him kneels a girl who is carefully taking a thorn out of his foot. At his side a smaller girl stands and wipes away his tears with her apron. Some bundles of sticks are lying on the ground near the children.

b. Four children, two girls and two boys, are seated at a table on which is an empty bird cage. Perched on a finger of the older boy is a bird which he is feeding. The younger boy holds out one of his fingers toward the bird. All the children are looking at the bird, and all are smiling.

c. A dog is lying on some hay in a manger, while an ox standing near is trying in vain to get at the hay.

[1] From "Modern Painters," by John Ruskin, Vol. I, Ch. II.

Chapter Four - Letter Writing

Lesson XIII - Social Letters

The charm of an informal social letter consists in its naturalness. We say in praise of such a letter from a friend, "It sounds as though he were here talking to us." All the model letters of Part I are of this kind.

A letter that is a natural expression of a writer's thoughts and feelings clearly reveals these thoughts and feelings, and the best way to make oneself capable of writing letters worth reading is to learn to think and to feel what is worth expressing.

Although the subject matter and the easy conversational style of a social letter are not governed by rules, the mere *form* of such letters is so governed.

In a social letter it is necessary to have the following parts: —

1. The heading.
2. The salutation.
3. The body of the letter.
4. The form of closing.
5. The signature.
6. The superscription.

The heading gives the place and the time of writing. Give the place with sufficient detail to enable your correspondent to address his letter to you properly. Begin the heading about an inch and a half from the top of the page.

Examples: —

50 Boylston Street,
Boston, Mass., June 15, 1902.
550 Monroe Avenue,
Chicago, Illinois, May 2, 1903.

The salutation varies with the writer's degree of intimacy with the person addressed. It is considered more formal to say "My dear —" than to say "Dear —." Write the salutation at the left on the line below the heading.

Examples: —
Dear Mary:
My dear Mr. Brown:
My dear Cousin:
Dear Father:
Dear Aunt Susan:
My dear Friend:

The form of closing also varies with the writer's degree of intimacy with the person addressed.

Begin it near the middle of the first line below the body of the letter.

Examples: —
Your loving daughter,
Your affectionate nephew,
Your grateful pupil,
Yours sincerely,
Very truly yours,
As ever, yours,

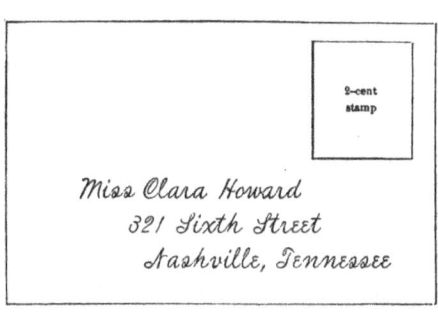

The superscription is what is written on the envelope. It should be placed as in the model given on this page. It is not necessary to use punctuation marks at the ends of the lines, except to mark abbreviations.

Written Exercises

1. Write a letter to a boy or a girl living in a foreign country, telling how you spend a day at school. You may, if you like, use the following outline: —

a. The getting ready for school.
b. The way to school.
c. The arrival.
d. The lessons.
e. The recesses.
f. The dismissal.

2. Write a letter to a classmate, giving an account of an excm:sion. Use the following outline: —

a. Preparations for an early start.
(Mention some difficulties that had to be overcome.)
b. The arrival at the boat.
c. The start.
d. Occupations of passengers.
e. The landing.
f. What was done on shore.
g. The return.

3. Write a letter to a friend in a distant city, giving an account of some interesting walk you have taken. The following outline is merely suggestive.

Crossing the New York and Brooklyn Bridge.

a. At the entrance in Manhattan. The crowds hurrying to the cars.
b. On the promenade.
   (1) The cars on either side.
   (2) The appearance of the bridge itself.
   (3) The view of the harbor.
   (4) The view of the East River.

4. Imagine yourself making a visit to some interesting foreign city, say Venice. Write to one of your classmates, giving an account of the journey and the arrival. It is expected that your reading about ocean travel and foreign countries will have given the information you need in writing this letter. Use the following outline: —

a. The departure.
   (1) The great vessel.
   (2) The farewells.
   (3) The start.
b. Life on shipboard.
   (1) The captain and the other officers.
   (2) The sailors.
   (3) The passengers.
c. Experiences on the Mediterranean.
   (1) Passing Gibraltar.
   (2) Arrival at Genoa.
d. The journey to Venice by train.
e. First glimpse of Venice (fairyland).
   (1) The gondolas at the railway station.
   (2) Traveling in a gondola along the Grand Canal.

Lesson XIV - Informal Notes

I

I wonder if you care to know how the great Beethoven looked! Even if you don't, I think the picture is interesting as a fine type of humanity, and I crave permission to add it to your collection of photographs. How strange it is that the greatest musician the world has ever seen should have been deaf to his own marvelous work and shut out from all sounds! Doesn't he look like a splendid old German lion, with a northeast hurricane in his hair? I haven't words to tell you how I admire him and his uplifting music.

From "Letters of Celia Thaxter." Edited by her friends A. F. and R. L.

II

Wimbledon, December 24, 1896.

My Dear ___,

I really don't know how to find words to thank you for the magnificent chair — nay, throne — which you have sent me, and which still overawes us all with its splendor. I hope by means of familiarity to get accustomed to the idea that it is for use, and a real seat to sit upon, and not an idol to which sacrifices of respect and admiration should be paid.

And now, as if that were not already too much, here comes in a noble turkey, fit for the biggest and the happiest Christmas table. I only wish the queen or some other distinguished person would pay us a visit, to sit in my chair and eat of my good cheer.

Abridged from "The Autobiography and Letters of Mrs. M. O. W. Oliphant." Edited by Mrs. Harry Coghill.

III

St. James' Place, August 17th, 1842.

My dear Tennyson,

Every day have I resolved to write and tell you with what delight I have read and read again your two beautiful volumes; but it was my wish to tell you so face to face. That wish, however, remains unfulfilled, and write I must, for very few things, if any, have ever thrilled me so much.

Yours ever,
S. Rogers.

From "Alfred, Lord Tennyson: A Memoir, by his son."

Study of the Models

A note is shorter than a letter proper, and is usually written for the purpose of expressing but one main thought. The first of these models is the body of a note sent with a gift. The writer has shown by her comments upon Beethoven's photograph that she has given some thought to the selection of the gift, thus making it more valuable to the receiver.

The second is part of a note expressing thanks for gifts received. The writer shows her appreciation of the gifts by the pleasant remarks about them which she makes.

The third note expresses one poet's appreciation of another poet's writings. It is only two sentences in length, but in the second sentence there is as much appreciation as could be expressed in a letter several pages long.

The six parts of an informal social note are usually placed as in a social letter (see preceding lesson). Sometimes the place at which the letter is written and the date are given after the note, at the end.

Written Exercises

1. Write a note of thanks for the gift of a book, telling why you like it.
2. Think of something you would very much like to own; imagine that a friend has given it to you; and write a note of thanks to this friend.
3. Write a note to accompany some old numbers of *St. Nicholas Magazine* and some of your picture books which you are sending to the children in a certain hospital.
4. Write a note to the author of your favorite book, telling him how much you like his writings. (Write the note, even if the author be no longer living.)
5. Write a note to your teacher, explaining why you cannot go to school today, and requesting her to tell you what to-morrow's lessons will be.

Lesson XV - Formal Notes

Mrs. Walter Cooke requests the pleasure of Miss Hamilton's company at dinner Thursday, January twenty-first, at seven o'clock.
  25 Ellison Street,
    February fifteenth.

Miss Hamilton regrets that a previous engagement prevents her accepting Mrs. Cooke's kind invitation for Thursday evening.
  16 Church Street,
    February seventeenth.

Mr. Huntoon accepts with pleasure Mrs. Cooke's kind invitation for Thursday evening.
  21 Eighteenth Street,
    February sixteenth.

Will Miss Wolfs be kind enough to excuse Arthur Frost from school at two o'clock this afternoon, and oblige his mother,
                                                                   Mary A. Frost.
  400 Carroll Street,
    Wednesday morning.

In formal notes no pronouns of the first or the second person are used. The name of the place at which the note is written is put at the end. If the date is written, it also is put at the end. In writing the dates, words are used instead of figures, and the year is usually not given. The spaces left blank at the top and the bottom of the page should be about equal.

Written Exercises

1. Write a formal note inviting a friend to luncheon.
2. Write a formal acceptance of an invitation to an evening reception.
3. Write in the name of your class a formal note inviting your principal to attend some special exercises to be held in your classroom.
4. Write in your mother's name a formal note to your teacher requesting her to excuse your absence from school.
5. Write a note accepting the following invitation: —
The Class of 1903 request the pleasure of Miss Lewis's company in the Assembly Room on Wednesday, June fifteenth, from four until six o'clock.

Lesson XVI - Business Letters

I

750 Tremont St.,
Boston, June 13, 1902.

Mr. John R. James,
Principal of Holmes School.
Dear Sir:
I regret to say that I am compelled to leave school and go to work.
I shall be greatly obliged if you will give me a letter of recommendation that will aid me in securing employment.

Respectfully yours,
Anna M. Smith.

II

150 East 28th St.,
New York, September 5, 1902.

James McCreery & Co.,
East Twenty-third St., New York.
Gentlemen:
In reply to your advertisement in the *New York Times* for a messenger boy, I beg leave to apply for the situation.
I am fourteen (14) years of age. I have completed the work in Grammar School No. 49. I inclose a letter of recommendation from Mr. Walter Raleigh, the Principal of that school.

Very respectfully,
John R. Mason.

III

12 Euclid Ave.,
Detroit, Mich., July 12, 1902.

American Book Co., Washington Square, New York.
Gentlemen:
  I inclose in this registered letter one dollar, for which please send me Matthews's "Introduction to the Study of American Literature,"

Respectfully yours,
George Gordon.

IV

Washington Square,
New York, July 13, 1902.

Mr. George Gordon,
  12 Euclid Avenue, Detroit, Mich.
Dear Sir:
  We are in receipt of your registered letter of July 12, inclosing one dollar and ordering a copy of Matthews's "Introduction to the Study of American Literature."
  The last edition of this book is exhausted. A new edition will be published in a few days, when a copy will be sent you.
  Thanking you for your order and regretting the unavoidable delay in filling it, we remain.

Respectfully yours,
American Book Co., Per J. L. R.

Study of the Models

In writing business letters be guided by the following directions: —

1. Write above the salutation the name and the address of the person or persons to whom the letter is written. To make the letter a little less formal these two items may be written after the letter, at the left.

2. In a letter to a woman use as the form of salutation "Madam" or "Dear Madam." In writing to a man use "Sir" or "Dear Sir." In writing to more than one man use "Sirs," "Dear Sirs," or "Gentlemen."

3. In a business letter an unmarried woman should prefix to her signature the title Miss, written in parentheses. A married woman should prefix to her signature the title Mrs. written in parentheses, or she should write in parentheses under her signature the title Mrs. followed by her husband's name.

4. In replying to a business letter mention the date of that letter and state briefly its contents. By doing this you save the time of your correspondent, and you prevent misunderstanding.

5. Make the body of the letter as brief as you can, but, at the same time, perfectly clear. In trying to be brief, do not be discourteous, and do not, because they are short, use incorrect forms of words. It is neither courteous nor correct to use such forms as *rec'd, y'rs,* or to omit the subjects of sentences. Never write, "Would say that, etc.," "Received your letter."

Written Exercises

1. Write a letter applying for a position as entry clerk; as stenographer and typewriter.
2. Write a letter to your Principal asking for a letter of introduction to the mayor of your city, or to the sheriff of your county.
3. Write a letter to the Treasurer of the Franklin Debating Society, inclosing the amount of your semi-annual dues.
4. Write a letter for the Treasurer of the Franklin Debating Society, calling upon a delinquent member to pay his dues.
5. Write a letter, inclosing $4 to Harper and Brothers, Franklin Square, New York, for a subscription for one year to *Harper's Monthly*.
6. Write a letter in reply to a letter from the Secretary of the Franklin Debating Society, inviting you to open a debate on a certain evening. State the subject of the debate.

Chapter Five - Versification

I

"Give me of your bark, O Birch tree!
Of your yellow bark, O Birch tree!
Growing by the rushing river.
Tall and stately in the valley!
I a light canoe will build me.
Build a swift Cheemaun for sailing,
That shall float upon the river,
Like a yellow leaf in autumn.
Like a yellow water-lily!'"

From "The Song of Hiawatha," by Henry W. Longfellow.

II

"Build me straight, worthy Master!
　Stanch and strong, a goodly vessel,
That shall laugh at all disaster.
　And with wave and whirlwind wrestle!"

From "The Building of the Ship," by Henry W. Longfellow.

III

Lives of great men all remind us
　We can make our lives sublime,
And, departing, leave behind us
　Footprints on the sands of time: —

    Footprints, that perhaps another,
        Sailing o'er life's solemn main,
    A forlorn and shipwrecked brother,
        Seeing, shall take heart again.
From "A Psalm of Life," by Henry W. Longfellow.

Study of the Models

In Lesson XX, Part I, you learned that in poetry the lines can be divided into measures or feet, and that a foot consisting of a short syllable followed by a long is called an iambic foot.

In each of the three extracts given in this lesson we have a different kind of foot. We will measure off the first line thus: —

    Give me | of your | bark, O | Birch tree!

Each measure has two syllables, a long and a short, but the long comes first. A measure of this kind is called a *trochaic* foot. Measure off the other lines of the first extract.

Observe that the extract from "The Building of the Ship" is also written in trochaic measure, with four feet to each line. But this extract differs from the first in having rhyme. The words *master* and *disaster* are considered correct rhymes because they have —

1. The same accented vowel sound (*a*),
2. The same sounds following the accented vowel (*ster*).
3. Different consonants preceding the accented vowel (*m* and *s*).

Show that *vessel* and *wrestle* have these three characteristics, and are therefore correct rhymes.

In the extract from "A Psalm of Life" the first and third lines of both stanzas have each four trochaic feet, but the other lines are different. We may measure one of them thus: —

    We should | make our | lives sub | lime.

Observe that the fourth foot has but one syllable. Its short syllable is lacking.

Rhyming lines should have the same indention; that is, they should be begun at equal distances from the margin of the page.

Exercises

1. Mark off in measures the syllables in the following verses. Note the arrangement of the rhyming lines.

    January, bleak and drear,
    First arrival of the year.
    Named for Janus — Janus who.
    Fable says, has faces two;
    Pray, is that the reason why
    Yours is such a fickle sky?
Frank Dempster Sherman.

Alone and warming his five wits.
The white owl in the belfry sits.

Alfred Tennyson.

Little drop of dew,
   Like a gem you are;
I believe that you
   Must have been a star.

Frank Dempster Sherman.

"The time has come," the Walrus said,
"To talk of many things:
Of shoes — and ships — and sealing-wax —
Of cabbages — and kings —
And why the sea is boiling hot —
And whether pigs have wings."

Lewis Carroll.

Who will shield the fearless heart?
   Who avert the murderous blade?
From the throng with sudden start,
   See, there springs an Indian maid.
Quick she stands before the knight:
   "Loose the chain, unbind the ring!
I am daughter of the king,
   And I claim the Indian right!"

From Thackeray's "Pocahontas."

My good blade carves the casques of men,
My tough lance thrusteth sure,
My strength is as the strength of ten,
Because my heart is pure.

From Tennyson's "Sir Galahad."

2. Write as many rhymes as you can think of for the following words: —
master year dew king time two star knight brother sky heart pure main sit blade men

3. Continue the following jingle, making each line consist of four trochaic feet with the fourth foot incomplete.

The Flowers' Mission

Flowers gay on shrub and tree,
O, how happy you must be!
Violets in glade and dell,
All the children love you well.
Clover blossoms in the field,
Sweetest honey you can yield.
Pansies smiling in the sun, etc.

Part III - Paragraphs

Chapter One - Indention

 The Great Stone Face was a work of nature in her mood of majestic playfulness, formed on the perpendicular side of a mountain by some immense rocks, which had been thrown together in such a position as, when viewed at a proper distance, precisely to resemble the features of the human countenance. It seemed as if an enormous giant, or a Titan, had sculptured his own likeness on the precipice. There was the broad arch of the forehead, a hundred feet in height; the nose, with its long bridge; and the vast lips, which, if they could have spoken, would have rolled their thunder accents from one end of the valley to the other.
 It was a happy lot for children to grow up to manhood or womanhood with the Great Stone Face before their eyes, for all the features were noble, and the expression was at once grand and sweet, as if it were the glow of a vast, warm heart, that embraced all mankind in its affections, and had room for more. It was an education only to look at it. According to the belief of many people, the valley owed much of its fertility to this benign aspect that was continually beaming over it, illuminating the clouds, and infusing its tenderness into the sunshine.
     Abridged from "The Great Stone Face," by Nathaniel Hawthorne.

Study of the Model

 You have only to glance at this selection to learn that it consists of two paragraphs. You know this because the first word of each paragraph is *indented,* that is, it begins a little farther to the right than the first words of the other lines of the paragraph. Because of this device of indention it is perfectly easy to tell, without reading a word, where a paragraph begins and where it ends. But to tell *why* a paragraph begins and ends where it does, is not at all easy, and only a careful reading will enable us to do it.
 Observe that the first of these paragraphs consists of three sentences which tell us in substance that —
 1. The Great Stone Face resembled a human face.
 2. It suggested the face of a giant.
 3. Its forehead, its nose, and its lips were all distinct.
 Now observe that these sentences are all concerned with the same thing; namely, the *appearance of the Great Stone Face.* We may say, therefore, that the first paragraph consists of a group of sentences treating the following topic: The appearance of the Great Stone Face.
 The substance of the three sentences of the second paragraph may be expressed as follows: —
 1. It was good for the people living in the valley to have the Great Stone Face continually before their eyes.

2. It was an education only to look at it.

3. Many people believed that its presence made the valley fertile.

Observe that these three sentences are all concerned with the same thing; namely, *the influence exerted by the Great Stone Face.* We may say, therefore, that the second paragraph consists of a group of sentences treating the following topic: The influence exerted by the Great Stone Face.

Now as both paragraphs are about the Great Stone Face, we may arrange their topics as follows: —

The Great Stone Face.
1. Its appearance.
2. Its influence.

From this analysis of the model we learn that a paragraph consists of a group of sentences treating a single topic. Only when we have said all that we mean to say about a topic, should we begin a new paragraph.

Exercises

1. In its original form each of the following selections had two paragraphs. Make two paragraphs of each selection, giving reasons for what you do.

a. If you looked at the mountain from the west, the line of the summit was wandering and uncertain, like that of most mountain tops; but seen from the east, the mass of granite showing above the dense forests of the lower slopes had the form of a sleeping lion. The flanks and haunches were vaguely distinguished from the mass; but the mighty head, resting with its tossed mane upon the vast paws stretched before it, was boldly sculptured against the sky. Long after the other parts of the hill country were opened to summer sojourn, the region of the Lion's Head remained almost primitively solitary and savage. A stony mountain road followed the bed of the torrent that brawled through the valley at its base, and at a certain point a still rougher lane climbed from the road along the side of the opposite height to a lonely farmhouse pushed back on a narrow shelf of land, with a meager acreage of field and pasture broken out of the woods that clothed all the neighboring steeps. The farmhouse level commanded the best view of Lion's Head, and the visitors always mounted to it, whether they came on foot, or arrived on buckboards or in buggies, or drove up in the Concord stages from the farther and nearer hotels.

From "The Landlord at Lion's Head," by W. D. Howells, Ch. L Harper & Brothers.

b. Oh! But he was a tight-fisted hand at the grindstone, Scrooge! a squeezing, wrenching, grasping, scraping, clutching, covetous old sinner! Hard and sharp as flint, from which no steel had ever struck out generous fire; secret, and self-contained, and solitary as an oyster. The cold within him froze his old features, nipped his pointed nose, shriveled his cheek, stiffened his gait; made his eyes red, his thin lips blue; and spoke out shrewdly in his grating voice. A frosty rime was on his head, and on his eyebrows and his wiry chin. He carried his own low temperature always about with him; he iced his office in the dog days; and didn't thaw it one degree at Christmas. No one ever stopped him in the street to say with gladsome looks, "My dear Scrooge, how are you? When will you come to see me?" No beggars implored him to bestow a trifle, no children asked him what it was o'clock; no man or woman ever once in all his life inquired the way to such and such a place of Scrooge. Even the blindmen's dogs appeared to know him; and when they saw him coming on, would tug their owners into doorways and up courts; and then would wag their tails as though they said, "No eye at all is better than an evil eye, dark master!"

From "A Christmas Carol," by Charles Dickens.

c. When I first opened my eyes upon my native town, it was nearly two hundred years old, counting from the time when it was part of the original Salem settlement, — old enough to have gained a character and an individuality of its own, as it certainly had. We children felt at once that we belonged to the town, as we did to our father or our mother. The sea was its nearest neighbor, and penetrated to every fireside, claiming close intimacy with every home and heart. The farmers up and down the shore were as much fishermen as farmers; they were as familiar with the Grand Banks of Newfoundland as they were with their own potato fields. Every third man you met in the street, you might safely hail as "Shipmate," or "Skipper," or "Captain."

From "A New England Girlhood," by Lucy Larcom, Ch. V.

d. There was but one summer holiday for us who worked in the mills, — the Fourth of July. We made a point of spending it out of doors, making excursions down the river to watch the meeting of the slow Concord and the swift Merrimack; or around by the old canal-path, to explore the mysteries of the Guard Locks; or across the bridge, clambering up Dracut Heights, to look away to the dim blue mountains. On that morning it was our custom to wake one another at four o'clock, and start off on a tramp together over some retired road whose chief charm was its unfamiliarity, returning to a very late breakfast, with draggled gowns and aprons full of dewy wild roses. No matter if we must get up at five the next morning and go back to our humdrum toil, we should have the roses to take with us for company, and the sweet air of the woodland which lingered about them would scent our thoughts all day, and make us forget the oily smell of the machinery.

From "A New England Girlhood," by Lucy Larcom, Ch. Vin.

e. Mr. Toil had a severe and ugly countenance, especially for such little boys or big men as were inclined to be idle; his voice, too, was harsh; and all his ways and customs seemed very disagreeable to our friend Daffydowndilly. The whole day long, this terrible old schoolmaster sat at his desk overlooking the scholars, or stalked about the schoolroom with a certain awful birch rod in his hand. Now came a rap over the shoulders of a boy whom Mr. Toil had caught at play; now he punished a whole class who were behindhand with their lessons; and, in short, unless a lad chose to attend quietly and constantly to his book, he had no chance of enjoying a quiet moment in the schoolroom of Mr. Toil. Now, the whole of Daffydowndilly's life had hitherto been passed with his dear mother, who had a much sweeter face than old Mr. Toil, and who had always been very indulgent to her little boy. No wonder, therefore, that poor Daffydowndilly found it a woeful change, to be sent away from the good lady's side, and put under the care of this ugly-visaged schoolmaster, who never gave him any apples or cakes, and seemed to think that little boys were created only to get lessons.

Abridged from "Little Daffydowndilly," by Nathaniel Hawthorne.

f. When New York was evacuated by the British troops, November 25, 1783, the condition of the city was miserable to the last degree. Streets which had been opened and partly graded before the war began, had been suffered to lapse again to idle wastes; the wharves, to which for so long a while no ships had come, had crumbled through neglect; public and private buildings, taken possession of by the military and used as barracks, as hospitals and as prisons, had fallen into semi-ruin; along all the western side of the town was the wreck left by the fire. In this dismal period the population had dwindled from upward of 20,000 to less than 10,000 souls; the revenues of the city, long uncollected, had shrunk almost to the vanishing point; the machinery of civil government had been practically destroyed. In a word, without the consoling glory of having suffered in honorable battle, the city was left a wreck by war. The brilliant rapidity with which New York revived from what seemed to be its dying condition, affords a striking proof of its inherent strong vitality. Within three years from the date of the evacuation the former population had been regained, and within five years more a further increase of 10,000 had made the total 30,000 souls. Commerce, likewise, had returned to, and then had passed, its former highest limit. Public and private enterprise once more had been fully aroused. In every way the energetic life and the material prosperity of the city had been more than regained.

From "In Old New York," by Thomas A. Janvier. Harper & Brothers.

2. In its original form each of the following selections consisted of but two paragraphs. Re-write each selection in two paragraphs. At the head of the selection place the topics of the paragraphs, as in the study of the model.

a. When water from rain or melted snow sinks below the surface into the soil, or into rock, it does not remain at rest there. If you were to dig a deep hole in the ground, you would soon find that the water which lies between the particles would begin to trickle out of the sides of your excavation, and gather into a pool in the bottom.

If you baled the water out, it would still keep oozing from the sides, and the pool would ere long be filled again. This would show you that the underground water will readily flow into any open channel which it can reach. Now the rocks beneath us, besides being in many cases porous in their texture, such as sandstone, are all more or less traversed with cracks — sometimes mere lines, like those of a cracked window-pane, but sometimes wide and open clefts and tunnels.

These numerous channels serve as passages for the underground water.

From "Physical Geography," by Archibald Giekie.

b, Perseus saw the three Gorgons sleeping, as huge as elephants.

He knew that they could not see him, because the hat of darkness hid him; and yet he trembled as he sunk down near them, so terrible were those brazen claws.

Two of the Gorgons were foul as swine, and lay sleeping heavily, as swine sleep, with their mighty wings outspread; but Medusa tossed to and fro restlessly, and as she tossed, Perseus pitied her, she looked so fair and sad.

Her plumage was like the rainbow, and her face was like the face of a nymph, only her eyebrows were knit, and her lips clinched with everlasting pain; and her long neck gleamed so white in the mirror, that Perseus had not the heart to strike, and said: "Ah, that it had been either of her sisters!"

Adapted from "The Heroes, or Greek Fairy Tales," by Charles Kingsley.

c. We had passed for some time along the wall of a park, and at length the chaise stopped at the gate.

It was in a heavy, magnificent old style, of iron bars fancifully wrought at top into flourishes and flowers. The huge square columns that supported the gate were mounted by the family crest.

Close adjoining was the porter's lodge, sheltered under dark fir trees and almost buried in shrubbery.

The postboy rang a large porter's bell, which resounded through the still frosty air, and was answered by the distant barking of dogs, with which the mansion house seemed garrisoned.

An old woman immediately appeared at the gate. As the moonlight fell strongly upon her, I had a full view of a little primitive dame, dressed very much in the antique taste, with a neat kerchief and stomacher, and her silver hair peeping from under a cap of snowy whiteness. She came curtsying forth, with many expressions of simple joy at seeing her young master.

From "The Sketch-Book," by Washington Irving.

Chapter Two - Unity

1. The great error in Rip's composition was an insuperable aversion to all kinds of profitable labor. 2. It could not be from the want of assiduity or perseverance; for he would sit on a wet rock, with a rod as long and heavy as a Tartar's lance, and fish all day without a murmur, even though he should not be encouraged by a single nibble. 3. He would carry a fowling piece on his shoulder for hours together, trudging through woods and swamps, and up hill and down dale, to shoot a few squirrels or wild pigeons. 4. He would never refuse to assist a neighbor, even in the roughest toil, and was a foremost man at all country frolics for husking Indian corn or building stone fences. 5. The women of the village, too, used to employ him to run their errands, and to do such little odd jobs as their less obliging husbands would not do for them: in a word, Rip was ready to attend to anybody's business but his own; but as to doing family duty, and keeping his farm in order, he found it impossible.

From "Rip Van Winkle," by Washington Irving.

Study of the Model

Read the model. Observe that the subject, or topic, of the paragraph is *Rip's aversion to all kinds of profitable labor.* Now consider each of the sentences in turn to see whether anything is treated that does not belong to this topic.

Sentence 1 simply states the topic. Sentences 2, 3, 4, and the part of 5 preceding the colon, tell us of different kinds of labor to which Rip was *not* averse. Is sentence 1 contradicted by the sentences that follow it? No, because, although fishing, hunting, running on errands, etc., were indeed forms of labor that demanded perseverance, they were not *profitable* to Rip. As the last clause of sentence 5 states, it was only profitable work, the work by which he might have earned his living, that Rip found it impossible to do.

By considering each of its sentences in this way, we find that there is nothing in the paragraph which does not relate to the single topic. *Rip's aversion to all kinds of profitable labor.* We may say, then, that this paragraph treats of this one topic and only of this one topic: hence, that it has *unity*.

Exercises

1. Taking each of the following paragraphs in turn, consider each sentence carefully, and be prepared to show, if called upon by your teacher, how it relates to the subject, or topic, written at the head of the paragraph. (Follow the plan used in the second paragraph of the *Study of the Model* in this chapter.)

My aunt's severe but handsome appearance

My aunt was a tall, hard-featured lady, but by no means ill-looking. There was an inflexibility in her face, in her voice, in her gait and carriage, amply sufficient to account for the effect she had made upon a gentle creature like my mother; but her features were rather handsome than otherwise, though unbending and austere. I particularly noticed that she had a very quick, bright eye. Her hair, which was gray, was arranged in two plain divisions, under what I believe would be called a mobcap; I mean a cap, much more common then than now, with sidepieces fastening under the chin. Her dress was of a lavender color, and perfectly neat; but scantily made, as if she desired to be as little encumbered as possible. I remember that I thought it, in form, more like a riding-habit with the superfluous skirt cut off, than anything else. She wore at her side a gentleman's gold watch, if I might judge from its size and make, with an appropriate chain and seals; she had some linen at her throat not unlike a shirt collar, and things at her wrists like little shirt wristbands.

From "David Copperfield," by Charles Dickens, Ch. XIII.

A safe and comfortable hiding-place

In Allan Water, near by where it falls into the Forth, we found a little sandy islet, overgrown with burdock, butterbur, and the like low plants, that would just cover us if we lay flat. Here it was we made our camp, within plain view of Stirling Castle, whence we could hear the drums beat as some part of the garrison paraded. Shearers worked all day in a field on one side of the river, and we could hear the stones going on the hooks and the voices and even the words of the men talking. It behooved to lie close and keep silent. But the sand of the little isle was sun-warm, the green plants gave us shelter for our heads, we had food and drink in plenty; and, to crown all, we were within sight of safety.

From "Kidnapped," by Robert Louis Stevenson, Ch. XXVI.

Skill required in catching a big trout

Send your fly in under those cedar branches, where the water swirls around by that old log. Now draw it up toward the foam. There is a sudden gleam of dull gold in the white water. You strike too soon. Your line comes back to you. In a current like this, a fish will almost always hook himself. Try it again. This time he takes the fly fairly, and you have him. It is a good fish, and he makes the slender rod bend to the strain. He sulks for a moment as if uncertain what to do, and then with a rush darts into the swiftest parl^ of the current. You can never stop him there. Let him go. Keep just enough pressure on him to hold the hook firm, and follow his troutship down the stream as if be were a salmon. He slides over a little fall, gleaming through the foam, and swings around in the next pool. Here you can manage him more easily; and after a few minutes' brilliant play, a few mad dashes for the current, he comes to the net, and your skillful guide lands him with a quick, steady sweep of the arm. The scales credit him with an even pound, and a better fish than this you will hardly take here in midsummer.

From "Little Rivers," by Henry Van Dyke.

2. Write a suitable subject, or topic, for each of the following paragraphs, being careful to frame one to which each sentence of the paragraph relates.

a. Like a shop foreman, who knows exactly where each tool is, and where the raw material is stored, John went without hesitation to a bunch of second growth in a near-by windfall and chose and cut two birch saplings whose main crotches were about six feet from the ground. He quickly cut and trimmed an armful of poles of various sizes, which Hardy helped to carry in. He planted the birch saplings in the duff, four feet apart, and drove them until the crotches were only four feet high. A short crossbar was put in? the crotches, and the facade was complete. Two strong poles, eight feet long, sloped from each crotch downward and backward, parallel to each other, to where they were embedded in the duff. A few poles were laid on this wedge-shaped frame to support the sheets of bark that were put on it. A sheet of bark was braced to each side and partly supported by a few armfuls of moss which were packed against them, and the one-night stand was complete. It was made by a man with an ax.

From "The Lovers of the Woods," by W. H. Boardman.

b. How much do dogs really understand of our language? Perhaps a good deal more than we generally imagine. Please observe that in learning a foreign tongue you arrive at a certain stage where most of what the foreign people say is broadly intelligible to you, and yet you cannot express yourself at all. Very young children understand a great deal before they are able to express themselves in words. Even horses — and horses are incomparably less intelligent than dogs — understand a complete vocabulary of orders. May not a dog of ability enter to some extent into the meaning of spoken language, even though he may never be able to use it?

From "Dogs," by Philip Gilbert Hamerton.

c. Abel Stebbins, the Doctor's man, took the true American view of his difficult position. He sold his time to the Doctor, and, having sold it, he took care to fulfill his half of the bargain. The Doctor, on his part, treated him, not like a gentleman, because one does not order a gentleman to bring up his horse or run his errands, but he treated him like a man. Every order was given in courteous terms. His reasonable privileges were respected as much as if they had been guaranteed under hand and seal. The Doctor lent him books from his own library, and gave him all friendly counsel, as if he were a son or a younger brother.

From "Elsie Venner," by Oliver Wendell Holmes.

d. A New England "mansion house" is naturally square, with dormer windows projecting from the roof, which has a balustrade with turned post round it. It shows a good breadth of front yard before its door, as its owner shows a respectable expanse of clean shirt front. It has a lateral margin beyond its stables and offices, as its master wears his white wristbands showing beyond his coat cuffs. It may not have what can properly be called grounds, but it must have elbowroom, at any rate. Without it, it is like a man who is always tight buttoned for want of any linen to show. The mansion house which has had to button itself up tight in fences, for want of green or gravel margin, will be advertising for boarders presently.

From "Elsie Venner," by Oliver Wendell Holmes.

e. I recall very fully the moment and the place when I first heard of Don Quixote....The moment was at the close of a summer's day just before supper, which, in our house, we had lawlessly late, and the place was the kitchen where my mother was going about her work, and listening as she could to what my father was telling my brother and me and an apprentice of ours, who was like a brother to us both, of a book that he had once read. We boys were all shelling pease, but the story, as it went on, rapt us from the poor employ, and whatever our fingers were doing, our spirits were away in that strange land of adventures and mishaps, where the fevered life of the knight, truly without fear and without reproach, burned itself out.

From "My Literary Passions," by W. D. Howells. Harper & Brothers.

f. A great autobiography is Benjamin Franklin's. Franklin had exactly the genius and temperament of an autobiographer. He loved and admired himself; but he was so bent upon analysis and measurement that he could not let even himself pass without discrimination. He watches his own life as he watched one of his own philosophical experiments. He flies his existence as he flew his kite, and he tells the world about it all just as a thoughtful boy might tell his mother what he had been doing — sure of her kindly interest in him. The world is like a mother to Ben Franklin always, so domestic and familiar is his thought of her. He who has read this book has always afterward the boy-man who wrote it clear and distinct among the men he knows.

Adapted from "Biography," by Phillips Brooks.

g. There is no more fascinating biography than the "Memoir of Professor Agassiz," which Mrs. Agassiz gave to the world a few months ago. It is the picture of a sweet, strong nature, turning in its first young simplicity to noble things, and keeping its simplicity through a long life by its perpetual association with them. It is a human creature loving the earth almost as we can imagine that a beast loves it, and yet at the same time studying it like a wise man. The sea and the glacier tell him their secrets. In his very dreams the extinct fishes build again for him their lost construction. There is a cool, bright freshness in every page. The boy of twenty-two rolls himself in the snow for joy. The man has himself let down a hundred and twenty-five feet into the cold, blue wonderful crevasse to see how the ice is made. Finally the New World tempts him, and he becomes the apostle of science to America. All this is told us out of the lips which have the best right to tell it.

Adapted from "Biography," by Phillips Brooks.

h. First-born among the Continents, though so much later in culture and civilization than some of more recent birth, America, so far as her physical history is concerned, has been falsely denominated the *New World.* Hers was the first dry land lifted out of the waters, hers the first shore washed by the ocean that enveloped all the earth beside; and while Europe was represented only by islands rising here and there above the sea, America already stretched an unbroken line of land from Nova Scotia to the Far West.

From "Geological Sketches," by Louis Jean Agassiz.

3. Write a paragraph about one of the following topics. You may, if you like, make use of the suggestions given with the topic.

a. Longfellow's love for his children. (Read the poem "The Children's Hour.")

Setting aside an hour for the children. Waiting for their coming. Pretending not to notice the plotting on the stairs. Enjoying the children's raid. b. How Robinson Crusoe worked for his bread.

(Read Chapter XII of "Robinson Crusoe.")

Turned ground with wooden spade. Sowed seed. Dragged a great bough over the ground to scratch the earth. Cut grain with cutlass. Rubbed it with his hands. Beat it in a wooden mortar with pestle of iron wood. Sifted the meal in sieves made of muslin. Baked the loaves in an oven made of an earthen vessel.

c. Snow statuary.

Proper condition of snow. Size of figures — large enough to last for several weeks after the snow has disappeared from the ground. Variety of subjects.

d. Choosing a dog.

Choice depends upon use to which he is to be put. Desirable qualities. Characteristics of certain kinds of dogs: poodle, good for tricks; Scotch terrier, intelligent; Newfoundland, faithful, powerful, companionable; spaniel, pretty, affectionate, docile; shepherd, trusty; bull terrier, good companion for a boy, — lively, intelligent, watchful, courageous.

e. The village blacksmith. (Read Longfellow's poem.)

His appearance — hands, arms, hair, face. His character — honest, industrious, pious, affectionate.

f. Outdoor games.

Changing with the seasons. Those especially adapted to girls or to boys. Favorites.

Chapter Three - Plan

From the listless repose of the place and the peculiar character of its inhabitants, who are descendants from the original Dutch settlers, this sequestered glen has long been known by the name of Sleepy Hollow, and its rustic lads are called the Sleepy Hollow Boys throughout all the neighboring country. A drowsy, dreamy influence seems to hang over the land and to pervade the very atmosphere. Some say that the place was bewitched by a High German doctor during the early days of the settlement; others, that an old Indian chief, the prophet or wizard of his tribe, held his powwows there before the country was discovered by Master Hendrick Hudson. Certain it is, the place still continues under the sway of some witching power that holds a spell over the minds of the good people, causing them to walk in a continual reverie. They are given to all kinds of marvelous beliefs, are subject to trances and visions, and frequently see strange sights and hear music and voices in the air. The whole neighborhood abounds with local tales, haunted spots, and twilight superstitions; stars shoot and meteors glare oftener across the valley than in any other part of the country, and the nightmare with her whole ninefold seems to make it the favorite scene of tier gambols.

From "The Legend of Sleepy Hollow," by Washington Irving.

Study of the Model

From what you learned in the last chapter you can easily find the topic of this paragraph, and can show that the paragraph has unity. Now, how has the writer managed to stick to his topic, admitting nothing that does not concern it, and stopping when he has said all that he means to say about it? He has followed a definite *plan*.

Let us try to discover this plan. We may consider the topic to be *the dreaminess of Sleepy Hollow and of its people.* Read the first two sentences of the paragraph. These tell you how the place and the people came to be named. Read the third sentence, and you will learn how some people accounted for the atmosphere of the place and the character of its people. Read from the sentence beginning "Certain it is," to the end of the paragraph, and you will learn how the spell supposed to be cast over the place by the German doctor or the Indian wizard acts — it makes the people dreamy and superstitious.

We may set down our plan as follows: — The dreaminess of Sleepy Hollow and of its people.
1. Derivation of the name.
2. Supposed cause of the general dreaminess,
    a. The High German doctor.
    b. The Indian wizard.
3. Effect of this dreaminess.
    a. The reveries of the people.
    b. The beliefs of the people.

Notice that the main divisions of the topic are marked by Arabic numerals and that the subdivisions are marked by the letters of the alphabet. The former may be called subtopics; the latter, sub-subtopics.

Exercises

1. Write an outline for each of the following paragraphs, setting down first, as in the model, the topic, and marking the subtopic by Arabic numerals, and the sub-subtopics by the letters of the alphabet.

a. There are very few moments in a man's existence when he experiences so much ludicrous distress, or meets with so little charitable commiseration, as when he is in pursuit of his own hat. A vast deal of coolness and a peculiar degree of judgment are requisite in catching a hat. A man must not be precipitate, or he runs over it; he must not rush into the opposite extreme, or he loses it altogether. The best way is, to keep gently up with the object of pursuit, to be wary and cautious, to watch your opportunity well, get gradually before it, then make a rapid dive, seize it by the crown, and stick it firmly on your head: smiling pleasantly all the time, as if you thought it as good a joke as anybody else.

From "Pickwick Papers," by Charles Dickens, Ch. IV.

b. In Washington were combined all the highest qualities of a general — dogged tenacity of purpose, endless fertility in resource, sleepless vigilance, and unfailing courage. No enemy ever caught him unawares, and he never let slip an opportunity of striking back. He had a rare geographical instinct, always knew where the strongest position was, and how to reach it. He was a master of the art of concealing his own plan and detecting his adversary's. He knew better than to hazard everything upon the result of a single contest, and because of the enemy's superior force he was so often obliged to refuse battle that some of his impatient critics called him slow; but no general was ever quicker in dealing heavy blows when the proper moment arrived. He was neither unduly elated by victory nor discouraged by defeat. When all others lost heart, he was bravest; and at the very moment when ruin seemed to stare him in the face, he was craftily preparing disaster and confusion for the enemy.

From "The War of Independence," by John Fiske, Ch. VI.

c. This child of my invention was nearly six feet square, exclusive of two triangular flaps to serve as a pillow by night and as the top and bottom of the sack by day. I call it "the sack," but it was never a sack by more than courtesy: only a sort of long roll, or sausage, green water-proof cart-cloth without and blue sheep's fur within. It was commodious as a valise, warm and dry for a bed. There was luxurious turning room for one; and at a pinch the thing might serve for two. I could bury myself in it up to the neck; for my head I trusted to a fur cap, with a hood to fold down over my ears and a band to pass under my nose like a respirator; and in case of heavy rain I proposed to make myself a little tent, or tentlet, with my water-proof coat, three stones, and a bent branch.

From "Travels with a Donkey," by Robert Louis Stevenson.

2. From each of the following outlines write a single paragraph.

a. Breaking-in a horse. (To write this from the horse's standpoint, read Chapter III of "Black Beauty.")

(1) What breaking-in means.
(2) The bit and the bridle.
(3) The saddle and the rider.
(4) The iron shoes.
(5) The harness — the blinkers, the crupper.
(6) Getting used to the passing of noisy vehicles.
b. Rules governing a snowball battle.
(1) Election of officers.
(2) Choice of position.
(3) Choice of men.
(4) Position of fort and camp.
(5) Kinds of balls used.
(6) Treatment of prisoners.
(7) Capture of enemy's colors.
c. The building of Hiawatha's canoe. (Read "Hiawatha's Sailing.")
(1) How the materials were obtained,
(*a*) Bark of birch.
(*b*) Boughs of cedar.
(*c*) Roots of larch.
(*d*) Resin of fir.
(*e*) Quills of hedgehog.
(2) How these materials were used.
d. The skipper's daughter. (Read Longfellow's "The Wreck of the Hesperus.")
(1) Her appearance.
(2) Her fear of the storm.
(3) Her bewilderment — the bells, the light.
(4) Her prayer.
(5) Her death.
e. The lives of moths and butterflies.
(1) Chief difference between a moth and a butterfly.
(2) Three stages of existence, (*a*) The caterpillar. (*b*) The chrysalis. (*c*) The perfect insect.

Chapter Four - The Topic Sentence

The first spring wild-flowers, whose shy faces among the dry leaves and rocks are so welcome, yield no honey. The anemone the hepatica, the bloodroot, the arbutus, the numerous violets the spring beauty, the corodalic, etc., woo all lovers of nature but do not woo the honey-loving bee. It requires more sun and warmth to develop the saccharine element, and the beauty of these pale striplings of the woods and groves is their sole and sufficient excuse for being. The arbutus, lying low and keeping green all winter, attains to perfume, but not to honey.

From "The Pastoral Bees," by John Burroughs.

When Longfellow read verse it was with a hollow, with a mellow, resonant murmur, like the note of some deep-throated horn. His voice was very lulling in quality, and at the Dante Club it used to have early effect with an old scholar who sat in a cavernous armchair at the corner of the fire, and who drowsed audibly in the soft tone and gentle heat. The poet had a fat terrier who wished always to be present at the meetings of the Club, and he commonly fell asleep at the same moment with that dear old scholar, so that when they began to make themselves heard in concert, one could not tell which it was that most took our thoughts from the Paradiso, When the duet opened, Longfellow would look up with an arch recognition of the fact, and then go gravely on to the end of the canto. At the close he would speak to his friend and lead him out to supper as if he had not seen or heard anything amiss.

From "My Literary Friends and Acquaintances," by W. D. Howells. Harper & Brothers.

The crows we have always with us, but it is not every day or every season that one sees an eagle. Hence I must preserve the memory of one I saw the last day I went bee hunting. As I was laboring up the side of a mountain at the head of a valley, the noble bird sprang from the top of a dry tree above me and came sailing directly over my head. I saw him bend his eye down upon me, and I could hear the low hum of his plumage, as if the web of every quill in his great wings vibrated in his strong, level flight. I watched him as long as my eye could hold him. When he was fairly clear of the mountain he began that sweeping spiral movement in which he climbs the sky. Up and up he went without once breaking his majestic poise till he appeared to sight some far-off alien geography, when he bent his course thitherward and gradually vanished in the blue depths.

From "An Idyl of the Honeybee," by John Burroughs.

Study of the Models

Read the first model. Observe that its subject, or topic, *is the absence of honey from the first spring wildflowers.* The topic is announced in the very first sentence. Because it states or suggests the topic, this sentence is called the topic sentence of the paragraph. When a topic sentence comes at the beginning of a paragraph, it prepares the reader for what is to follow. In some paragraphs the topic sentence does not come until the end. In such cases it usually serves to sum up what has been said.

Read the second model. Observe that its topic is *an illustration of Longfellow's gentle manners,* but in no sentence is this topic stated. Thus we see that although every paragraph has a subject, or topic, not every paragraph has the topic stated in one of its sentences, and therefore not every paragraph has a topic sentence.

Read the third model. Observe that the writer of this paragraph gives an account of his seeing an eagle. The topic of the paragraph is stated in the second sentence. All the sentences that follow the second help to give this account. But why are *crows* mentioned in the first sentence? Does not the first clause of the first sentence seem out of place? It would be out of place if it were not true that in the composition from which this paragraph is taken something is said about crows in the preceding paragraph. We thus see that this allusion to crows serves to connect the two paragraphs. Sometimes only a word is used to establish the connection between paragraphs. Read the paragraph from "The Legend of Sleepy Hollow" on page 170. What is the use of the word *however* in the first line?

Exercises

1. Write an outline of each of the following paragraphs.
2. Copy the topic sentences of such of the paragraphs as have topic sentences.

a. My sister had a trenchant way of cutting our bread-and-butter for us, which never varied. First, with her left hand she jammed the loaf hard and fast against her bib — where it sometimes got a pin into it, and sometimes a needle, which we afterward got into our mouths. Then she took some butter (not too much) on a knife and spread it on the loaf, in an apothecary kind of way as if she were making a plaster — using both sides of the knife with a slapping dexterity, and trimming and molding the butter off round the crust. Then she gave the knife a final smart wipe on the edge of the plaster, and then sawed a very thick round off the loaf: which she finally, before separating from the loaf, hewed into two halves, of which Joe got one, and I the other.

From "Great Expectations," by Charles Dickens, Ch. II.

b. The sun, the great awakener of life, the king of nature, shoots his burning rays every day athwart the face of the waters. He causes the invisible vapors to rise, which, lighter than the air itself, unceasingly tend to soar into the atmosphere, filling it and constituting within it another aqueous atmosphere. In their ascending movement, they encounter the colder layers of the higher regions of the atmosphere, which perform the part of coolers. They are condensed in vesicles, that become visible under the form of clouds and fogs. Then home along by the winds, whether invisible still or in the state of clouds, they spread themselves over the continents, and fall in abundant rains upon the ground which they fertilize. All the portion of the atmospheric waters not expended for the benefit of the plants and of the animals, nor carried off anew into the atmosphere by evaporation, returns by the springs and rivers to the ocean, whence it came.

From "The Earth and Man," by Arnold Guyot.

c. On the last day of 1775, England came within an ace of losing Quebec. At two o'clock in the morning, in a blinding snowstorm, Montgomery and Arnold began a furious attack, at opposite sides of the town; and, aided by the surprise, each came near carrying his point. Montgomery had almost forced his way in when he fell dead, pierced by three bullets; and this so chilled the enthusiasm of his men that they flagged, until reinforcements drove them back. Arnold, on his side, was severely wounded and carried from the field; but the indomitable Morgan took his place, and his Virginia company stormed the battery opposed to them, and fought their way far into the town. Had the attack on the other side been kept up with equal vigor, as it might have been but for Montgomery's death, Quebec must have fallen. As it was, Morgan's triumphant advance only served to isolate him, and presently he and his gallant company were surrounded and captured.

From "The American Revolution," by John Fiske, Ch. IV.

d. The proof-reading of the *Atlantic Monthly* was something almost fearfully scrupulous and perfect. The proofs were first read by the under proof reader in the printing office; then the head reader passed them to me perfectly clean as to typography, with his own abundant and most intelligent comments on the literature; and then I read them, making what changes I chose, and verifying every quotation, every date, every geographical and biographical name, every foreign word to the last accent, every technical and scientific term. Where it was possible, or at all desirable, the proof was next submitted to the author. When it came back to me, I revised it, accepting or rejecting the author's judgment, according as he was entitled by his ability and knowledge or not to have them. The proof now went to the printers for correction; they sent it again to the head reader, who carefully revised it and returned it again to me. I read it a second time, and it was again corrected. After this it was revised in the office and sent to the stereotyper, from whom it came to the head reader, for a last revision in the plates.

From "Literary Friends and Acquaintances," by W. D. Howells, Part IV. Harper & Brothers.

e. After serving two terms as President, George Washington returned to private life at Mount Vernon. He had been for more than twenty years the foremost man of the country in the eyes of the world. When he left the Presidency, he made a Farewell Address to the people of the United States. In that address, which is weighty with wisdom, he urged the people to prize the Union which they had formed. He bade them remember that each part of the country had free intercourse with all the other parts, and that each could help the others. He begged them to suffer no parties to rise within the Union which should weaken its strength, and he called on them to glory in the name of American. He reminded them that Europe had interests with which America had little concern. "Extend your business relations with Europe," he said in effect, "but do not be dragged into her politics. Do not suffer yourselves to have passionate attachments for other nations. Be strong in yourselves, and you will be independent of the Old World."

From "A New History of the United States," by Horace E. Scudder, Ch. IX.

f. I would not have it imagined, however, that he [Ichabod Crane] was one of those cruel potentates of the school, who joy in the smart of their subjects; on the contrary, he administered justice with discrimination rather than severity, taking the burden off the backs of the weak, and laying it on those of the strong. Your mere puny stripling, that winced at the least flourish of the rod, was passed by with indulgence; but the claims of justice were satisfied by inflicting a double portion on some little, tough, wrong-headed, broad-skirted Dutch urchin, who sulked and swelled and grew dogged and sullen beneath the birch. All this he called "doing his duty by their parents"; and he never inflicted a chastisement without following it by the assurance, so consolatory to the smarting urchin, that "he would remember it, and thank him for it, the longest day he had to live."

From "The Legend of Sleepy Hollow," by Washington Irving.

3. Complete the paragraphs suggested by the following topic sentences: —

a. No winter sport is more exciting and amusing than snowball warfare.

b. Whittier's barefoot boy knows many things that he did not learn at school.

c. Hiawatha could do wonders with his magic mittens and his magic moccasins.

d. It is easy to see why the daisy should have been called the "day's eye."

e. An indoor window-garden can be made to bloom all the year round.

f. The life of birds is beset with dangers.

g. Hawthorne's "Wonder Book" is a wonder book indeed!

h. It does not take much of a person's time to take care of a canary bird.

i. Some of the rhymes that children sing when they play are very entertaining.

Part IV

Chapter One - Description

From the study of certain of the models m the preceding parts of this book we have learned the following: —

A description sets forth the appearance and qualities of things. It is a picture made by means of language.

We write a description in order to make others see a certain thing as we see it and feel about it as we feel.

In describing we should carefully select the points to be mentioned, making no reference to the points that will not help to produce the impression we wish to make on our readers.

After deciding what points we shall mention in our description, we should arrange these points in proper order. In other words, we must have a plan.

In planning descriptions we should mention first the thing that first attracts our attention when we see the object. We should mention next the thing that would be noticed next.

In order to enable another person to see with his mind's eye what we are describing, it is sometimes well to use comparisons.

Oral Exercises

Selection. With whose eyes does Hawthorne let us look at Grandfather s Chair (Part I)? Why does he make no mention of the arms, the legs, the seat, and the cushion, in his description? Why has Miss Alcott not selected corresponding features in describing the four "little women" (Part I)? Can you tell from the descriptions how the author wishes us to feel toward each of the sisters? With whose eyes are we supposed to be looking at East's study (Part I)? Why are so many details given in the description? Why do you believe that Charles Dudley Warner, even if he had noticed some unsightly objects on the shores of the Bras d'Or, would not have mentioned them in his description (Part I)? Why in his description of a century-old portrait does George William Curtis tell so much concerning the costume (Part I)? Why does Bayard Taylor not tell us about the number, the sizes, and the titles of the books in the library at Vienna (Part I)? With whose eyes does Hawthorne let us see the toyshop window (Part I)?

Can you show how he is guided in his selection of details by his knowledge of little Annie's tastes? How does David Copperfield by his selection of details in describing his aunt show that her appearance was both severe and handsome (Part III)? How does Whittier in the description from "Snow Bound" in Part III, show that the familiar landscape had become an unknown world?

Plan. Why is the bright appearance of Grandfather's Chair mentioned first in the description (Part I)? In what order are the other details mentioned? What does the first paragraph of *East's Study* tell about the impression which the room made upon Tom Brown (Part I)? Why is the size of the room mentioned before other details? In what order are the other features mentioned? Is this the order in which one who was carefully examining the room would probably notice these things? What does the first sentence in the description of the Bras d'Or tell about the way in which the lake impressed the beholder (Part I)? Why was it a good plan to begin the detailed description of the lake with a reference to the map? After drawing the reader's attention to the situation of the lake, was it natural for the writer to mention next the irregular shore-line? In what order are the other details given? Would the first glance at the portrait described in Part I tell the beholder that it represented a "young and blooming girl"? In what order are the details of the description given? How and where does the writer tell us that the impression he received from the portrait was one of peacefulness — serenity? If a person stood where he could see the whole of the long hall described in Part I, what would probably be the first thing to attract his attention? What would he notice next? In what order are the other details of the description given? Where does the description proper end and the writer's reflections begin? What does the sentence "Is this a toyshop or is it fairyland" tell about the impression the toyshop window makes upon little Annie (Part I)? How would the details of this description differ in arrangement if the writer's purpose were to make a picture of the window similar to the picture of East's study on page 33?

Comparisons. In what respect did the oak of Grandfather's chair resemble mahogany (Part I)? Why did Jo remind one of a colt (Part I)? Why are the bluebirds compared to actors, in Part I? What comparisons are used in "An Underground Flower" (Part I)? Does it help you in forming a picture of the sack described in Part III to be told that it resembled a sausage?

Written Exercises

1. *a.* Mention in order the details given in the following descriptions. (Outline the plans just as you would if the extracts were in prose.) *b.* Write the descriptions in prose, following your own outlines.

> And, when the second morning shone.
> We looked upon a world unknown.
> On nothing we could call our own.
> Around the glistening wonder bent
> The blue walls of the firmament.

No cloud above, no earth below, —
A universe of sky and snow!
The old familiar sights of ours
Took marvelous shapes; strange domes and towers
Rose up where sty or corncrib stood,
Or garden wall, or belt of wood;
A smooth white mound the brush pile showed,
A fenceless drift what once was road;
The bridle post an old man sat
With loose-flung coat and high cocked hat;
The well curb had a Chinese roof;
And even the long sweep, high aloof.
In its slant splendor, seemed to tell
Of Pisa's leaning miracle.
       From "Snow Bound," by Whittier.

 Patroclus then in glittering brass
Arrayed himself; and first around his thighs
He put the beautiful greaves, and fastened them
With silver clasps; around his chest he bound
The breastplate of the swift Aeacides,
With starlike points, and richly chased; he hung
The sword with silver studs and blade of brass
Upon his shoulders, and with it the shield
Solid and vast; upon his gallant head
He placed the glorious helm with horsehair plume,
That grandly waved on high. Two massive spears
He took, that fitted well his grasp, but left
The spear which great Achilles only bore,
Heavy and huge and strong, and which no arm
Among the Greeks save his could poise.
       From the "Iliad," Book XVI.

 In the Acadian land, on the shores of the Basin of Minas,
Distant, secluded, still, the little village of Grand Pré
Lay in the fruitful valley. Vast meadows stretched to the eastward.
Giving the village its name, and pasture to flocks without number.
Dikes, that the hands of the farmers had raised with labor incessant.
Shut out the turbulent tides; but at stated seasons the floodgates
Opened, and welcomed the sea to wander at will o'er the meadows.
West and south there were fields of flax, and orchards and cornfields
Spreading afar and unfenced o'er the plain; and away to the northward
Blomidon rose, and the forests old, and aloft on the mountains
Sea fogs pitched their tents, and mists from the mighty Atlantic
Looked on the happy valley, but ne'er from their station descended.
There, in the midst of its farms, reposed the Acadian village.
       From "Evangeline," by Longfellow.

2. Make a list of the details you would mention in describing (*a*) the exterior of the house in which you live; (*b*) the view from a certain window; (*c*) a street car; (*d*) an unabridged dictionary; (*e*) an elephant; (*f*) a plant.

3. Bring to class descriptions found in your reading of (*a*) a person; (*b*) a place; (*c*) an object.

4. Describe the lake represented in the picture on this page. (Read the description of Loch Katrine in Scott's "Lady of the Lake," Canto I, xiv.)

Loch Katrine

Chapter Two - Narration

Narration is the setting forth in some intended order of real or imaginary happenings.

The simplest form of narration is without plot; that is, its parts are not arranged so as to arouse the reader's interest concerning the way in which the narration will end. In a narration of this kind it is only necessary to select events that are interesting and to narrate them clearly and simply in the order in which they occurred. Unless a writer is himself interested in the event he is narrating, it is not likely that he will interest his readers.

Another form of narration is one that has a plot. In a narration of this kind the parts are arranged so as to arouse the reader's interest concerning the way in which the story will end, or the way in which things will turn out. No matter how simple the plot is, there is always some incident more important than the other incidents. This main incident is called the climax of the story. Everything else in the story should lead up to this main incident or should result from it.

A story may have besides its plot, a purpose; that is, it may teach a lesson. In Aesop's fables the purpose is plainly seen; but a story may be told so skillfully that it may teach the reader an important truth without appearing to do more than narrate a series of interesting events.

What helps to make some stories interesting is the dialogue in them. Dialogue should not be used for its own sake; it should help to tell the story. A dialogue that is well written usually reveals something concerning the characters of the persons who are supposed to be talking.

The writer of a good historical narrative does three things; namely, —

1. He studies in order to learn all the facts of the case.
2. He puts himself in the places of the actors.
3. He so tells the story as to make the event he narrates seem as real to his readers as it seems to himself.

Oral Exercises

Plot. What is the plot of "The Judicious Father" (Part I)? What is its main incident or climax? Could you so relate the incident of Julian Hawthorne's fall into the brook (Part I), as to make it the climax of a story — a story somewhat similar to Lucy Larcom's in Part I? Although the fable in Part I is told to teach a lesson, has the story a plot? In telling the story of the colt, outlined in Part I, what would you make the climax? The story of the stolen horse, outlined in Part II? What is the plot of Hans Andersen's story in Part II? What is its main incident? Would you end the story of little Johannes (Part I) by letting an accident happen to the boy as a punishment for his disobedience? If you did this, what would the description in the first paragraph have to do with the main incident? Does not this description and the description in the third paragraph of the story seem to be leading up to a less matter-of-fact climax — to something more in the nature of a fairy tale?

Purpose. What lesson might other ten-year-old girls learn from the extract given in Part I? Did the writer of the diary have any intention of teaching a lesson? What does the fourth paragraph of An Accident (Part I) teach concerning the beliefs of the author of "A New England Girlhood"? If you should invent the story of "Meddlesome Matty" suggested in Part I, what truth concerning conduct would you have it embody? What lesson is taught by the story of Dilly-dally (Part I)? What truths about animal life are illustrated by the story of the colt in Part I, the story of the ducklings in Part I the story of the stuffed owl in Part II, and the story of the wise horse in Part II? If you should complete the story of little Johannes (Part I) by letting an accident happen to him, what truth about conduct would you be illustrating? What lesson is taught by the story suggested by the picture entitled Feeding her Chickens? By the anecdote (*b*) in Lesson VI, Part II? By Hans Andersen's story The Teapot, on Part II? How are the virtues of courage and patriotism illustrated in The Death of Wolfe? What truth is taught by the poem on this page?

Written Exercises

(*a*) Outline the plots of the following narrations,
(*b*) From your outlines write the stories in prose.

This I beheld, or dreamed it in a dream: —
There spread a cloud of dust along a plain;
And underneath the cloud, or in it, raged
A furious battle, and men yelled, and swords
Shocked upon swords and shields. A prince's banner
Wavered, then staggered backward, hemmed by foes.
A craven hung along the battle's edge, and thought,
"Had I a sword of keener steel —
That blue blade that the king's son bears, — but this
Blunt thing —! "He snapt and flung it from his hand,
And lowering crept away and left the field.
Then came the king's son, wounded, sore bestead.
And weaponless, and saw the broken sword,
Hilt buried in the dry and trodden sand.
And ran and snatched it, and with battle-shout
Lifted afresh, he hewed his enemy down,
And saved a great cause that heroic day.

Edward Rowland Sill.

In mediaeval Rome, I know not where,
There stood an image with its arm in air,
And on its lifted finger, shining clear,
A golden ring with the device, "Strike here!"
Greatly the people wondered, though none guessed
The meaning that these words but half expressed.
Until a learned clerk, who at noonday
With downcast eyes was passing on his way.
Paused, and observed the spot, and marked it well.
Whereon the shadow of the finger fell;
And, coming back at midnight, delved, and found
A secret stairway leading underground.
Down this he passed into a spacious hall,
Lit by a flaming jewel on the wall;
And opposite in threatening attitude
With bow and shaft a brazen statue stood.
Upon its forehead, like a coronet.
Were these mysterious words of menace set:
"That which I am, I am; my fatal aim
None can escape, not even yon luminous flame!"
Midway the hall was a fair table placed.
With cloth of gold, and golden cups enchased
With rubies, and the plates and knives were gold.
And gold the bread and viands manifold.
Around it, silent, motionless, and sad.
Were seated gallant knights in armor clad.
And ladies beautiful with plume and zone.
But they were stone, their hearts within were stone;
And the vast hall was filled in every part

With silent crowds, stony in face and heart.
Long at the scene, bewildered and amazed,
The trembling clerk in speechless wonder gazed;
Then from the table, by his greed made bold,
He seized a goblet and a knife of gold,
And suddenly from their seats the guests upsprang,
The vaulted ceiling with loud clamors rang.
The archer spread his arrow, at their call.
Shattering the lambent jewel on the wall.
And all was dark around and overhead; —
Stark on the floor the luckless clerk lay dead!

Longfellow.

Chapter Three - Exposition

Exposition, or explanatory composition, is the setting forth of the nature and relations of a substance, a class of objects, or an idea.

In description we tell how a thing looks, in narration we tell how something happened, but in exposition we explain the meaning of a thing. To understand how exposition differs from description and narration, you have only to read again some of the model expositions in this book; for example, *How to Play Tee-Tah-Toe* (Part I), *How to Make and Manage a Float* (Part I), *Invalids' Food* (Part I), *Learning to Swim* (Part I), *Winter Fishing* (Part I), *Dogwatches* (Part II), *The Camp Fire* (Part II).

Even when we ourselves see clearly what a thing means we cannot always make the meaning clear to others; we may know perfectly how to do a thing, but we cannot always tell others how to do it. (See Lesson VIII, Part I.) Hence, in writing expositions, even more than in writing descriptions and narrations, is it necessary to follow a carefully constructed plan.

The first thing to do in making a plan of a composition is to put down the topics you mean to treat. These topics must be kept distinct; that is, they should not run into one another. They should all have a direct bearing on the subject of the composition; in other words, the composition should have unity. They should follow one another naturally — the first should suggest the second, the second the third, and so on.

After the main divisions have been set down, the subdivisions may be made. As each main division represents a paragraph, its subdivisions should be planned as suggested in Part III, Ch. 3.

Divisions of the same rank should be expressed in similar forms. For example, if in a certain outline the first main division is expressed in the form of a sentence, the other main divisions should be in sentences also; if it is in the form of a phrase, the others should be phrases in form.

The usual method of designating topics in an outline is to use Roman numerals for the main divisions, Arabic numerals for the subdivisions, and small letters for the sub-subdivisions. When there is but one division of a topic, it should not be numbered at all.

Following is the outline for an exposition which illustrates the rules for planning given above.

Kinds of Compositions

i. Description.
  1. What it is.
  2. Why it is written.
  3. How it is written.
    a. Details are selected with a special purpose in view.
    b. These are arranged in the natural order of observation.
  4. How it makes use of comparisons.
II. Narration.
  1. Definition.
  2. Kinds.
    a. Without plot.
    b. With plot.
  3. Purpose, or lessons taught.
  4. Use and treatment of dialogue.
  5. Special treatment of historical narrative.
III. Exposition.
  1. What it is.
    How it differs from description and narration.
  2. How it is planned.
    a. Divisions of subject.
    b. Expression of these divisions.
    c. Designation of divisions.

Written Exercises

1. Write an exposition on "Kinds of Composition," using the outline described above.

2. From the following outlines write expositions.

The Paragraph

I. What it is.
II. How it is indented.
III. What it must have.
  1. Unity.
    a. What this means.
    b. An illustration.
  2. Plan.
    a. What this means.
    b. An illustration.

Versification

I. Measures, or feet.
  1. Iambic.
    a. Definition.
    b. Illustration.
  2. Trochaic.
    a. Definition.
    b. Illustration.
II. Rhyme.
  1. Definition.
  2. Illustration.
  3. Make a similar outline for an exposition of some topic selected from your recent school work.

Chapter Four

Lesson I - Clearness

Whether a composition be a description, a narration, or an exposition, it should be *clear*; that is, it should express the writer's meaning in a way that cannot be misunderstood. The sentence exercises at the ends of most of the lessons in Part I were given for the purpose of training you to express your thoughts with clearness.

Lack of clearness is sometimes due to —

i. Poor judgment in choosing words, especially in choosing between synonyms — words having nearly the same meaning. (For exercises, see Part I.)

II. Violation of the rules of punctuation. The most important rules of punctuation are given in Appendix I.

III. Violation of the rules of grammar. Following are some of these rules that are frequently disregarded: —

1. Do not omit words that are necessary to the sense. (For exercises, see Part I, Lesson I.)

2. Make subject words and their predicate verbs agree in person and number.

3. Do not use a pronoun of whose antecedent the reader may not be certain (Part I).

4. Use the possessive form of a noun or pronoun that modifies a gerund (verbal noun) (Part I).

5. Use the objective forms of pronouns after transitive verbs and prepositions (Part I). Use the nominative forms after verbs expressing mere state of being.

6. In a clause expressing a condition which you know to be contrary to fact, use a verb in the subjunctive mode (Part I).

7. Use *shall* with the first person, and *will* with the second and third persons to express mere futurity. Use *will* with the first person and *shall* with the second person to express purpose or determination. In questions use *shall* with the first person, but, with the second and third persons, use the form you expect in the answer (Part I).

8. Place word, phrase, and clause modifiers where there can be no doubt as to what you intend them to modify (Part I).

Exercises

a. Observe each pair of italicized words used in the following sentences, and tell what meaning they have in common and what meaning is peculiar to each.

b. Make original sentences, using the pairs of words.

1. Fifty cents of John's money was spent for a knife and the *remainder* for a pencil. The merchant's *balance* at the bank was small.

2. If a man's *character* is what it should be, he can afford to let his *reputation* take care of itself.

3. The rules of syntax were *discovered* and stated by grammarians, they were not *invented* by them.

4. Mr. A. had no business dealings with this *person*. He would not be a, *party* to the transaction.

5. *Let* me alone, I want to read. Do not *leave* me here alone.

6. You will not continue to be *healthy,* if you do not eat *healthful* food.

7. *Take* your books home this afternoon, but *bring* them here to-morrow.

8. Shall you be glad when you have written the *last* exercise in this book? What was the subject of your *latest* composition?

9. This color is not *quite* like that, but the two materials are *somewhat* similar.

10. All persons are *liable* to make mistakes. You are not *likely* to fail in a lesson that you have carefully studied.

11. I shall go *unless* I am prevented, but I will not go *without* you.

12. *Most* boys like history. *Almost* every girl can learn to sing.

13. Why were you *angry* this morning? Are all the inmates of an insane asylum *mad*?

14. By *observation* you can learn much about the habits of animals. The *observance* of the Sabbath was general in colonial New England.

15. *Shall* I do that for you? *Will* you do this for me?

16. *Shall* you be at school to-morrow? *Will* you come to my house this afternoon?

17. John *shall* learn his lessons — I will attend to the matter. James *will* learn any lesson you give him, for he likes to study.

18. The money could not have been divided into equal *parts*, for the two sons did not receive equal *portions*.

19. The children laughed at the clown's *funny* stories. It is *odd* that the news of my misfortune should have come to me in this way.

20. After the boy had walked *into* the stream he continued to walk *in* the water.

Lesson II - Emphasis

When we write about a subject we are, or should be, much interested in it, and we should wish to make our readers interested in it also. To interest others we must write not with clearness only but with *emphasis* as well. Most of the exercises at the ends of the lessons in Part II are given to train you to write with proper force, or emphasis.

In speaking we may emphasize important words by uttering them with considerable stress, but in writing we cannot use this mode of emphasizing. Some writers print words in italics in order to let the reader know that these words are emphatic, but this is usually an unnecessary thing to do because sentences may be so worded and their parts so arranged as to show readers where the emphasis belongs.

Some common ways of making expressions emphatic are these: —

1. By making statements in the exclamatory or interrogative form instead of the declarative. (For exercises, see Part II, Lesson III.)

2. By using the direct instead of the indirect method of reporting another person's words (Part II, Lesson VI).

3. By placing certain parts of a sentence out of their ordinary or regular positions; for example, by placing a subject after its predicate, or by placing an adverb, an object, or an attribute at the beginning of the sentence. (The two most emphatic positions in a sentence are the beginning and the end. When the main part of a sentence is kept for the end, the modifying phrases and clauses being put at the beginning, the sentence is said to be periodic. When the main part of the sentence is put first, the sentence is said to be loose.) (Part II, Lessons VII and VIII.)

4. By using words that produce the vivid effect of reality (Parts I and II).

5. By telling what a thing is not in order to show what it is (Part II, Lesson XI).

Both clearness and emphasis are sometimes largely dependent upon the mere form of the sentences we use. Instead of writing only short simple sentences or compound sentences consisting of members connected by and we should learn to use properly the simple sentence containing participial or other phrases, the complex sentence, and the compound sentence containing conjunctions that express exactly the relation existing between the divisions of a thought. To be able to subordinate one part of a sentence to another we must know what is the principal part of the thought to be expressed and what, therefore, should be made the principal part of the sentence.

Written Exercises

Improve the following paragraphs by combining such of the sentences as should be combined.

1. The yearly festival was always kept at Plumfield. It was kept in the old-fashioned way. Nothing was allowed to interfere with it. For days beforehand the girls helped Asia and Mrs. Jo. They helped in the storeroom and kitchen. They helped to make pies and puddings. They helped to sort fruit. The boys hovered on the outskirts of the forbidden ground. They sniffed the savory odors. They peeped in at the mysterious performances. They were occasionally permitted to taste some delicacy in the process of preparation.

2. The Middle River gracefully winds through the valley. It winds over a sandy bottom. It sometimes sparkles in shallows. Then it gently reposes in the broad bends of the grassy banks. In one of these bends we tried our skill. Here the stream swirled around in seductive eddies. We heroically waded the stream. We threw our flies from the highest bank. Neither in the black water nor in the sandy shallows could any trout be coaxed to spring to the deceitful leaders. The meadows were sweet with the newly cut grass. The wind softly blew down the river. Large white clouds sailed high overhead. They cast shadows on the changing water. To all these gentle influences the fish were insensible. They sulked in their cool retreats.

3. The room was about five feet six inches long. It was five feet wide. It was seven feet high. This room Martin called his den. Several books occupied the shelves in the room. Some of these books were tattered. Others were in a much better state of preservation. The table was entirely occupied by a machine. It was an electric machine. From this Martin liked to administer small shocks to small boys. These boys were rash enough to venture into his study. The walls of the room were adorned by a small hatchet. They were adorned by a pair of climbing-irons. They were adorned also by Martin's tin candle-box. In this box he was endeavoring to raise a hopeful family of field mice.

4. Pleasant Pond is an irregular sheet of water. It is two miles or more in its greatest diameter. Maine waters are for the most part dark-complexioned, Indian-colored streams. Pleasant Pond is a pale-face among them. It is this both in name and in nature. It may be called a silver lake. Its waters seem almost artificially white and brilliant. Its waters are of remarkable transparency.

5. An English sparrow brought to his box a goose-feather. It was a large fine feather. He deposited his prize. He chattered his gratulations over it. Then he went away in quest of his mate. His next-door neighbor was a female bird. She saw her chance. She quickly slipped in and seized the feather. She did not carry it into her own box. She flew with it to a near tree. She hid it in a fork of the branches. Then she went home. When her neighbor returned with his mate she was innocently employed about her own affairs. The proud male found his feather gone. He came out of his box in a high state of excitement. With wrath in his manner and accusation on his tongue, he rushed into the cot of the female. He did not find his feather there. He stormed around awhile. He abused everybody in general and his neighbor in particular. Then he went away as if to repair the loss. As soon as he was out of sight, the shrewd thief went and brought the feath-

er home. She lined her own domicile with it.

Lesson III - Figures of Speech

There are certain forms of expression which give not only clearness and emphasis to what we say but beauty also. These are called *figures of speech*. The danger in using figures of speech is that we may try by means of them to get beauty without clearness or emphasis. A sentence that lacks clearness and vigor cannot possibly possess any real beauty.

The figures of speech most commonly used and most easily understood are: —

I. **Simile.** — When Hawthorne says that the oak of Grandfather's Chair shone like *mahogany* (Part I), he makes a comparison and nothing more, for he merely likens one thing to another of the same kind. But when Hiawatha says (Part II) that his canoe shall float upon the river —

> Like a yellow leaf in autumn.
> Like a yellow water-lily,

he compares things of different kinds — a boat with a leaf and a flower. By means of this comparison he tells us clearly, forcibly, and beautifully that his canoe shall move easily, lightly, and gracefully. A comparison of this kind is called a *simile*. A simile is an expressed comparison between objects of different kinds.

II. **Metaphor.** — When we say of a man, "His bark is worse than his bite," we mean simply that his words are more disagreeable than his acts, but we seem to be speaking of him as though he were a dog. If we said, "His words are worse than his acts, just as a dog's bark may be worse than his bite," we should be using a simile. Instead, however, of *expressing* a comparison in our first sentence, we merely *implied* one, and the figure we used is a *metaphor*. A metaphor is an implied or suggested comparison. Similes are employed to make language clearer, but metaphors usually make language more forcible. Metaphors often add beauty to an expression because the implied comparison suggests a beautiful image. Of this class is "Thy word is a lamp unto my feet."

III. **Personification.** — When the merchant bids the shipbuilder build him a vessel (Part II).

> "That shall laugh at all disaster.
> And with wave and whirlwind wrestle,"

he is using a metaphor, for he speaks of a vessel as if it were a strong, brave man. But this metaphor is also an example of personification; that is, it represents an inanimate thing as having the characteristics of a *person*. Personification ascribes to its object qualities of something higher than itself in the scale of being.

Exercises

1. Examine the following similes, and tell wherein the resemblance lies.
   a. Like silent ghosts in misty shrouds
   Stand out the white lighthouses high.
   Celia Thaxter.

   b. But now his nose is thin,
      And it rests upon his chin
      Like a staff.
   Holmes.

   c. Bead from some humbler poet,
      Whose songs gushed from his heart.
      As showers from the clouds of summer,
      Or tears from the eyelids start.
   Longfellow.

   d. As when a forest on the mountain top
      Is in a blaze with the devouring flame
      And shines afar, so, while the warriors marched.
      The brightness of their burnished weapons flashed
      On every side and upward to the sky.
   The "Iliad."

   e. Then, as the goatherds, when their mingled flocks
      Are in the pastures, know and set apart
      Each his own scattered charge, so did the chiefs,
      Moving among them marshal each his men.
   The "Iliad."

2. *a.* Examine the following metaphors and tell wherein the resemblance lies. *b.* Try to give, without using figurative language, the thoughts expressed by the sentences.
   Example: —
      "Thy mother is shaking the dreamland tree,
      And down comes a little dream on thee."

   b. Your mother is rocking you and singing to you, and now you are going to sleep.
   a. My school roof is the dappled sky;
      And the bells that ring for me there
   Are all the voices of morning
      Aloft in the dewy air.
   Kind Nature is the Madame;
      And the book whereout I spell
   Is dog's-eared by the brooks and glens
      Where I know the lesson well.
   Fitz-Hugh Ludlow.

   b. Among the beautiful pictures
      That hang on Memory's wall,

Is one of a dim old forest,
  That seemeth the best of all.

                                                        Alice Cary.

c. I have you fast in my fortress.
  And will not let you depart.
But put you down into the dungeons
  In the round tower of my heart.

                    From Longfellow's "The Children's Hour."

d. By a street called By-and-by you reach a house called Never.

e. Speech is silver, silence is gold.

f. Self-love is a mote in every man's eye.

g. A grain of prudence is worth a pound of craft.

h. Use your wit as a buckler, not as a sword.

3. Give, without using personification, the thoughts expressed in the following sentences.

Example. The treetops lash the air with sounding whips. — Longfellow.

The wind shakes the treetops so violently that they make a noise like sounding whips.

a. And then came autumn, with his immense burden of apples, dropping them continually from his overladen shoulders as he trudged along.

                                                               Hawthorne.

b. There's a dance of leaves in that aspen bower:
    There's a titter of winds in that beechen tree;
  There's a smile on the fruit, and a smile on the flower,
    And a laugh from the brook that runs to the sea.

                                                               Bryant.

c. A wind came up out of the sea,
  And said, "O mists, make room for me."

                                                            Longfellow.

d. The ocean old,
  Centuries old.
  Strong as youth, and as uncontrolled.
  Paces restless to and fro.
  Up and down the sands of gold.

                                                            Longfellow.

e. Aloft on the mountains sea fogs pitched their tents.

f. Oh, a dainty plant is the ivy green.
    That creepeth o'er ruins old!
  On right choice food are his meals, I ween.
    In his cell so lone and cold.
  The walls must be crumbled, the stones decayed.
    To pleasure his dainty whim;
  And the moldering dust that years have made.
    Is a merry meal for him.

                                                         Charles Dickens.

Chapter Five - Versification

You have learned that poetry is divided into measures, or feet, and that a measure consisting of a short syllable, followed by a long is called an iambic foot, while a measure consisting of a long syllable followed by a short is called a trochaic foot.

Some feet consist of three syllables instead of two. Let us examine the following lines of Whittier's: —

> 'Tis the moon of the springtime, yet never a bird
> In the wind-shaken elm or the maple is heard.

The accented syllables of the first line are *moon, spring, nev,* and *bird.* Those of the second are *wind, elm, ma,* and *heard.* The measures in each line may be indicated thus, the curves representing short syllables and the straight lines long: —

$$\smile\smile\_|\smile\smile\_|\smile\smile\_|\smile\smile\_$$

A foot consisting of two short syllables followed by one long syllable is called an *anapestic* foot.

Another kind of foot consisting of three syllables is found in the following lines from Tennyson: —

> Cannon to right of them,
> Cannon to left of them.

The accented syllables of the first line are *can* and *right*; those of the second are *can* and *left*. The measures in each line may be indicated thus: —

Observe that here it is the first rather than the last of the three syllables that is accented. A foot consisting of one long syllable followed by two short syllables is called a *dactylic* foot.

It frequently happens that there are two kinds of feet in one line. In the following, from Lowell, the first and fourth feet are iambic while the second and third are anapestic: —

> And what is so rare as a day in June?

Exercises

1. Mark off in anapestic feet the syllables of the following stanzas. (Observe that in most of the lines the first foot has only two syllables.)

> Oh, young Lochinvar has come out of the West!
> Through all the wide Border his steed is the best;
> And, save his good broadsword, he weapons had none;
> He rode all unarmed and he rode all alone.
> So faithful in love, and so dauntless in war,
> There never was knight like the young Lochinvar!   Scott.

Ah! on Thanksgiving day, when from East and from West,
From North and from South come the pilgrim and guest,
When the gray-haired New-Englander sees round his board
The old broken links of affection restored,
When the care-wearied man seeks his mother once more,
And the worn matron smiles where the girl smiled before,
What moistens the lip and what brightens the eye?
What calls back the past, like the rich Pumpkin pie?

Whittier.

2. Mark off in dactylic feet the syllables of the following selections. (Observe that in some of the lines the last foot has not three syllables.)

Far in the Northern Land,
By the wild Baltic's strand,
I, with my childish hand.
   Tamed the gerfalcon;
And, with my skates fast-bound,
Skimmed the half-frozen Sound,
That the poor whimpering hound
   Trembled to walk on.

Longfellow.

Merrily, merrily, shall I live now
Under the blossom that hangs on the bough.

Shakspere.

3. Write the following in the form of a stanza having five iambic feet to each line. For the rule as to the indention of rhyming lines, see page 137.

March

I Martins am! Once first, and now the third! To lead the year was my appointed place; a mortal dispossessed me by a word, and set there Janus with the double face. Hence I make war on all the human race; I shake the cities with my hurricanes; I flood the rivers and their banks efface, and drown the farms and hamlets with my rains.

4. Write the following as one stanza of trochaic couplets (pairs of rhyming lines). Fill the blanks with the missing rhyming words.

Who shall sing to bleak November; month of frost and glowing ember? Is there nothing then to praise in these thirty chilly ___? Ah, but who shall lack for song when the nights are still and ___; when beside the logwood ___ we may hear the wood-elves' choir, making dainty music float up the big brick chimney's ___!

5. Write the following in four stanzas of four lines each, the second and fourth lines rhyming.

A Summer Night

Night comes with arms extended, and to her breast the woods and fields and meadows are gently pressed. She softly folds her mantle the trees around, and lulls the world to slumber with bells' low sound. The earth, all care forgetting, in stillness lies; to heights above, beyond me, I lift my eyes. I see a bird dive into the sunset glow. — Would that my soul could follow where he may go!

6. Complete the following nursery rhymes as though you were writing them to entertain children.

Pennies

Pennies round, pennies red, —
   John had ten.
He spent them for a pencil-box
   And a new pen.

Pennies round, pennies red, —
   Kate had nine.
And for her mother dear she bought
   A new clothes-line.

Pennies round, pennies red.
   ___ ___ eight.
     etc.

Three Meals

Yesterday for breakfast
   I had an apple red,
Oatmeal, cream, and sugar,
   $\smile - \smile - \smile$ bread.
Yesterday for dinner
   I had a piece of steak,
Potatoes white, and gravy brown,
   $\smile - \smile - \smile -$
Yesterday for supper, etc.

A Pleasant Dream

I dreamt last night there came to me
   A fairy kind and sweet.
She said she liked my workbox small,
   It was so clean and neat;
So everything therein she changed
   To something good to eat.

Behold a little cake was where
   My pincushion had been,
A raisin stuck in every place
   Where there had been a pin.

(It made me glad to think I had
   A mouth to put it in.)
And of my little spools of thread
   With which I sew my seams, etc.

7. Complete the following fable: —

The Fox and the Grapes

A fox once saw some tempting grapes Upon a trellis high;
And said, "Those grapes are good, I'm sure; To get them I will try."

        ⌣—⌣—⌣—⌣—
          ⌣—⌣ might and main
        ⌣—⌣—⌣—⌣—
          ⌣—⌣— in vain.

        ⌣—⌣—⌣—⌣—
          ⌣—⌣—⌣ say,
        ⌣—⌣—⌣—⌣—
          ⌣—⌣ anyway."

8. Write in verse another of Aesop's fables or a fairy tale.

Appendix I - Rules for Punctuation, Capitalization, and Spelling

Note. — These rales are taken, with some slight modifications, from those given in Maxwell and Smithes "Writing in English," which in turn are adapted and condensed from Maxwell's "Advanced Lessons in English Grammar," pp. 270-278 (punctuation); pp. 69-76 (rules for use of capitals and for spelling).

I. Punctuation

Punctuation is necessary to mark (1) the close of a sentence; (2) pauses required in reading; (3) the elements or parts of sentences to be joined in meaning.

Terminal points. — The points used to mark the completion of a sentence are the period (.), the question mark (?), and the exclamation mark (!).

The *period* marks the *end* of every declarative and every imperative sentence, unless the words are spoken with strong feeling; then the exclamation mark is used; as, Go at once!

The *period* is also used to mark *abbreviations;* as. The Rev. John Sinclair, D.D., read from Rev. xxi.

The *question mark* is used after an interrogative sentence, and after a direct question contained in any sentence; example of the latter: When he asked, "What are you going to do about it?" we made no reply.

The *exclamation mark* is used after declarative and imperative sentences expressing strong feeling, commonly after interjections, and after the nominative of address when strong feeling is to be indicated; as, John! John! What a mess you have made! Oh dear! What shall I do?

Never place together a question mark and a period, or an exclamation mark and a period. Use one or the other.

Points within a sentence. — The points used within a sentence are the comma (,), the semicolon (;), the colon (:), the dash (—), quotation marks (" "), the parentheses [()].

The comma is used —

1. To separate the *nominative of address* from the rest of the sentence; as, Cassius, thou art yoked with a lamb.

2. To mark the *beginning of a direct quotation* (but see also the rules for the use of the colon); as. The judge said, "Gentlemen of the jury, what is your verdict?" If the quotation is not a question, and precedes the clause on which it depends, it is followed by a comma; as, "We are unable to agree," answered the foreman. If the clause on which a quotation depends is inserted between

parts of the quotation, it is cut off by two commas; as, "We have," said the foreman, "been unable to agree; but, if your Honor will let us have a little more time, we may be able to reach a conclusion."

3. To separate a very *long subject* from its verb; as, Whatever you may wish to do about this matter of answering his letter, will be agreeable to me. Here the subject is the whole clause, and not *letter* or *answering*, as might be carelessly supposed. In general, however, *a single comma is not to be used between the subject and the verb.*

4. To cut off, at its beginning and at its end, a *parenthetical* or explanatory expression. This includes —

Thrown-in words, like *however, to be brief, finally, besides, indeed, in fact, moreover.*

Nouns in apposition, especially when they are accompanied by modifiers; as, John Brown, the leader of the attack, was executed.

Relative clauses, when they are not restrictive but coordinate; as, John Brown, who led the attack, was executed.

Adjective and adverbial elements when they are inserted for explanation; as, General Wolfe, wounded and dying, learned of his great victory. That story is, in several particulars, improbable.

Adverbial clauses, when inserted for explanation; as, He determined that, if the chance were given him, he would set out for the Philippines at once.

5. An adverbial phrase, placed, for the sake of emphasis, before the subject of a sentence, is followed by a comma; as, Beyond the shadow of the ship, I watched the water snakes.

6. To separate words in *series,* conjunctions being omitted; as, Poetry, music, painting, and sculpture are not the only fine arts. He was tall, broad-shouldered, muscular, and active.

7. To separate words in *pairs,* for the same reason; as. The flower and the star, the pebble and the mountain, the raindrop and' the sea, all are the work of His hand.

8. To separate *clauses in a compound sentence*, when they are related in meaning, and are not themselves subdivided by commas; as. The rivulet becomes a brook, and the brook becomes a creek, and the creek becomes a river.

9. The omission of a predicate verb is indicated by a comma; as. To err is human; to forgive, divine.

10. When the same object follows two or more prepositions, a comma is inserted after each preposition; as, He was sent by, and he acted for, the people of the village.

The *parentheses* are used —

To inclose a remark that might be omitted without destroying the sense of the sentence; as, Know then this truth (enough for man to know), virtue alone is happiness below.

The *quotation marks* are used —

1. To inclose direct quotations. If a quotation includes another, the latter is inclosed in single inverted commas, to distinguish it from the main quotation, which is inclosed in the double inverted commas; as, "Aha!" said my lord, "I go on the principle that 'a bird in the hand is worth two in the bush.'"

2. Sometimes to indicate titles of books, and nicknames.

The *dash* is used —

1. To mark an abrupt turn in a sentence; as, I will tell you — but no! why should I not keep my own counsel?

2. To mark a significant pause that should be made in reading; as. Now you listen to what I have to say — I will never give you what you demand!

3. To mark words in apposition, or other parenthetical expressions; as, This work was performed four hundred years ago, and — such is the merit of good work — it endures to this day.

As a rule, it is better usage to set off parenthetical expressions by commas, than to set them off by dashes or parentheses.

The *semicolon* is used —

1. To separate the clauses of a compound sentence, when one or all of the clauses are subdivided by commas; as, Having detained you so long already, I shall not trespass longer on your patience; but, before concluding, I wish you to observe this truth.

2. To mark the beginning of an illustration introduced by *as* or *namely*, which should be followed by a comma. The following is an example: An island is a portion of land surrounded by water; as, Australia, Iceland.

The *colon* is used most commonly as follows: —

1. To indicate that a list, enumeration, or statement is to follow; as. The following are the principal rules for punctuating the possessive case: First, etc. Under this rule comes the use of a colon before a direct quotation, when the quotation is to be marked as especially emphatic; as, The dealer then uttered these words: "I believe you have been trying to cheat me. I refuse to deal with you at all."

2. In a long complex or compound sentence, after groups of clauses, or sometimes phrases, when the groups are separated by semicolons; as. If the man walked slowly, the lion lessened his pace; if the man stopped, the beast did likewise: but in spite of this seeming imitation of the man's movements, the lion was gradually gaining.

3. After the salutation at the beginning of a letter, particularly a business letter; as. Dear Sir: I am in receipt of your letter of June 18. Gentlemen: I beg leave to call your attention to the fact, etc.

Miscellaneous Marks

(1) The apostrophe (') is used to mark the omission of a letter when the abbreviated word is to be pronounced as it is spelled; as, don't, o'clock, o'er.

The apostrophe is a necessary part of all *nouns in the possessive case*, singular or plural. The rules for writing the possessive case are as follows: —

1. Nouns in the singular number add 's to the nominative form, whether the nominative ends in s or not; as, the man's, Charles's, Dickens's, Mr. Jones's, mouse's.

2. In the plural, if the nominative plural does not end in *s* or the sound of *s*, the apostrophe and *s* are added; as, men's, children's.

But if, as is usual, the plural already ends in *s*, only the apostrophe is added; as, girls' hats, the Joneses' house.

In short, to form the possessive, always add *'s*, except in the plural when the nominative plural ends in *s*.

In certain expressions, as, for goodness' sake, for conscience' sake, the *s* is omitted because there are already two *s* sounds present.

The pronouns *ours, hers, yours, its, theirs,* are written without any apostrophe.

(2) The *hyphen* (-) is used to connect the parts of a compound word, as, cathedral-tower; also to separate a word into its syllables. Usually this is necessary only at the end of a line where there is room for only a part of a word. A word of one syllable should never be written part on one line and part on the next. Words of more than one syllable should always be divided between syllables. For instance, to write alw-ays, or believ-ed, is wrong. In general, divide words so that the part beginning the next line shall begin with a consonant; as, re-quired, enumeration (not -ation). However, to divide before the syllable -ing, when it is preceded by a single consonant, is proper; as, follow-ing, eat-ing.

(3) The *caret* (^) is used to mark an error of omission in one's writing. It has been called the "blunder mark."

(4) Marks like * † ‡ § and others are used to direct attention to a note in the margin or elsewhere.

(5) *Underscoring* a word <u>once</u> indicates that it should be printed in italics; twice, in small capitals; three times or more, in large capitals, as for headings or title pages.

II. Use of Capital Letters

Begin with capitals —

1. The first word of every sentence, and of every line of poetry.

2. Every proper noun, every proper adjective (as French, Latin), every personified common noun (as. Then Peace shall smile upon us).

3. Every name or title of the Deity, pronouns pertaining to the Deity (this rule is to be followed with judgment; sometimes the repeated use of capitalized pronouns becomes tiresome and annoying), and names of religious denominations.

4. The names of the days of the week, the months of the year (but not the four seasons of the year, except when personified), and the four points of the compass when they denote great regions or sections of a country; as, He

journeyed west and north till he had traversed the region called the great Northwest.

5. The important words in the title of a book or of an essay or of a poem. (This is the rule generally followed. Many writers, however, capitalize only the first word in a title, unless a capital is required by one of the other rules.)

6. Titles of honor or respect; as, The Honorable Member from Ohio; the Duke of Westminster; His Excellency, the Governor of North Carolina; His Honor, the Mayor.

7. Words to be particularly emphasized, such as words denoting an important epoch of history; as, The period of the Thirty Years' War.

8. The first word of a direct quotation, except when only a word, a phrase, or a clause is quoted and made a part of the writer's own sentence.

9. Write with capitals the pronoun I and the interjections O, Oh.

III. Rules for Spelling

1. Final e silent is generally *omitted* before a *suffix beginning with a vowel*; as, write, writ-ing; please, pleas-ing, pleas-ure; grieve, griev-ance; combine, combining; change, changing; slice, slicing. But since c and g have the "hard" sound before a, o, and u, the endings ce and ge must be retained before suffixes ending in a, o, u. Thus, courageous, serviceable, changeable. The word singeing retains the e to distinguish it from singing; dyeing to distinguish it from dying. Shoeing and agreeable would be apt to be mispronounced if spelt shoing and agreable.

2. Final e is generally *retained* before a *suffix beginning with a consonant*; as, pale, paleness; dole, doleful. (Exceptions to this rule are judgment, acknowledgment, wholly, truly, and nursling.)

3. Words ending in a *single* consonant preceded by a single vowel, *double* the final letter on taking a suffix beginning with a vowel, if the words are *monosyllabic or accented on the last syllable.* Thus, begiń, begińning; sit, sitting; underpinning, repellent, befitting. But if the words are accented on some other than the last syllable, or if the consonant is preceded by two vowels, the consonant is not doubled; as, trav'el-er, viv'id-est, of'fer-ing, wor'ship-er, prof'it-ing, fo'cus-ing, bi'as-ed; retaining, toiling, revealing.

4. Words ending in a *double consonant* usually retain it when *suffixes* are added; as, ebb, ebbing; will, willful; shrill, shrillness. (But note the exceptions, — almost, altogether, also, although, fulfill, belfry, welfare.)

5. Words ending in a double consonant usually retain it when *prefixes* are added; as, farewell, downfall, respell, undersell. (Note the exceptions, — until, and adjectives ending in *-ful.*)

6. *Final y*, if preceded by a *consonant*, is usually changed to *i* when a suffix is added which begins with a vowel (except the suffix *-ing*); as, happy, happiest, happiness; fly, flies; rely, reliance; accompany, accompaniment; very,

verily; duty, dutiful. (Duteous, beauteous, and plenteous are not formed according to the rule.)

7. *Final y,* preceded by a *vowel*, or before the suffix *-ing*, is retained; as, valley, valleys; monkey, monkeys; spy, spying; pity, pitying.

Appendix II - Hints to Teachers on the Correction of Compositions

The chief object the teacher should keep in view in criticising a pupil's composition, is to make the pupil an intelligent critic of his own work. It is not enough that the child should memorize, or even that he should understand, the rules of grammar and rhetoric; he must be able to use them. If he is to master the art of composition, if he is to become able to use it freely and accurately in the everyday affairs of life, he must learn to test his work by the rules he has learned, he must acquire the habit of detecting and correcting his own errors.

Nor is this a habit that is easy of acquisition. Experience shows that, without this habit, children will commit the most flagrant breaches of rules with which they are perfectly familiar, and that even when errors are laboriously corrected by the teacher, the pupils will make the same mistakes over and over again. They will cling to the "and habit," they will put pronouns in the wrong case and verbs in the wrong number, they will neglect to paragraph, or they will make a paragraph of every sentence, and so on through the various categories of literary errors.

The prevalent method of criticising children's compositions does little or nothing to correct the faults of carelessness, to make the child the critic of his own work. The teacher does the work which the pupil ought to do. The teacher states the changes that should be made; the pupil perfunctorily makes the changes. The teacher's task is laborious and unprofitable; the pupil's task is uninteresting and mechanical. The teacher spends weary hours that ought to be devoted to study or recreation, in reading and marking compositions; the pupil becomes confirmed in habits of carelessness, because he finds his errors corrected without effort on his own part.

If, on the other hand, the pupil is required to find his own errors and to amend them as well as he can, he gradually acquires facility in the process, and, what is more to the purpose, he learns, while writing, to avoid faults previously committed and corrected. To a child so trained, the principles and rules of grammar and rhetoric are not a meaningless jargon of words, but canons, the most practical and the most interesting, of the most practical and the most interesting of all the arts — the art of composition.

Rules for training pupils to criticise and correct their own compositions may be comprehensively stated as follows: —

1. *The pupil should have free access to all needful hooks of reference.* These include (*a*) books of information regarding the subject matter, such as books on geography, history, travel, and the like; and (*b*) technical books on English, such as a dictionary, a grammar, a book of synonyms. To acquire the habit of turning rapidly to the proper book of reference and finding the exact information needed at the moment, is one of the most useful habits a child may acquire in school.

2. *The pupil should look for only one class of errors at one time.* To look for all kinds of errors at the same time is a task too bewildering for the immature mind of an elementary school, or even of a high school, pupil. His vigilance is not equal to the labor of detecting at one reading omissions and wrong arrangements in subject matter, offences against unity and clearness in paragraph and sentence structure, and mistakes in spelling, grammar, and composition. Hence it follows that a pupil, to criticise his own composition effectively, must read it several times, each time with a distinct purpose in view. The following order of readings is suggested: —

(*a*) The pupil should read his composition for the purpose of determining whether his outline has been properly followed. He should see that all omissions in subject matter are supplied, that mistakes of fact are corrected, that each chief division of the outline is embodied in a single paragraph, and that the sentences in each paragraph follow one another in natural order.

(*b*) The next reading may be devoted to sentence structure. He should correct each sentence that is lacking in unity or that offends against the rules of grammar. He should improve each sentence that violates the rules for clearness and strength.

(*c*) A third reading may be given to correcting errors in spelling, capitalization, and punctuation.

But here a word of caution is necessary. A system of criticism that is too elaborate, is unwise in the earlier years of school life. In the seventh and eighth years of the elementary school, the pupil should be able to pursue all the lines of investigation suggested above. Prior to the seventh year the teacher must be guided by the stage of the pupil's development in determining what kinds of errors the latter shall be called upon to detect and correct.

While, if the pupil is to become the successful critic of his own work, he must have constant practice in finding and correcting mistakes, it does not follow that the teacher is to abandon the field of criticism. In the first place, during the hour set apart for correction, each pupil should be encouraged, when in doubt, to appeal to his teacher for advice. Such appeals, when wisely answered, will give the teacher abundant opportunity for directing the young critic in his labors. In the second place, the teacher will find it prudent to look over his pupils' corrections to see that the work is neither shirked nor carelessly performed. Eternal vigilance on the part of the teacher is the price of painstaking work on the part of the pupil.

Throughout all stages of the composition lesson — the preparation, the writing, the criticism — the thought should be kept prominently before the mind of the pupil, that he is writing, not for the teacher's eye alone, but to instruct and entertain his classmates. To read a composition aloud in class should be the reward for work conspicuously well done. To achieve this distinction should become the ambition of every child. With this idea in mind he will find delightful the task that once was irksome, and will feel the joy of giving pleasure to others.

Under no circumstances should the teacher rewrite a pupil's composition, either in whole or in part. He should simply point out errors which the pupil should correct. To lighten the labor of this work he should adopt a code of marks that will be easily understood by his pupils. These marks should, as a rule, be placed in the margin, while the words referred to are underscored in the body of the text. The following [1] are suggested: —

Amb. Ambiguous; word or expression may be understood in more than one way.
Arr. Arrangement faulty, causing lack of clearness or lack of emphasis.
C. Capital required or wrongly used.
Ch. Choice of word poor. Cl. Lack of clearness.
Cond. Condense; cut out unnecessary words, phrases, or even sentences.
Gr. Mistake in grammar.
Inc. Incomplete; necessary part of sentence omitted.
Mis. Misstatement of fact.
N. Lack of neatness.
P. Bad pronunciation.
Po. Wrong position of words.
O. Outline disorderly or badly arranged.
Om. Omission of necessary word or words.
Quot. Use direct quotation for emphasis and punctuate accordingly.
Red. Redundancy; use of superfluous words or unnecessary repetition of an idea.
Rew. Rewrite.
S. Bad spelling.
T. Topic of paragraph not clear.
Tr. Transpose.
V. Unity, either of sentence or of paragraph, violated.
¶ Make a paragraph.
No ¶ Do not paragraph.
^ Some letter, word, or words, omitted (mark to be used in the body of the text, not in the margin).
(-) Hyphen lacking or word wrongly divided.

[1] The marks given above are taken, with some omissions, from Maxwell and Smith's "Writing in English."

www.ingramcontent.com/pod-product-compliance
Lightning Source LLC
Chambersburg PA
CBHW031648040426
4243CB00006B/250